IMAGES OF ENGLAND

# PORTSMOUTH AT WAR

IMAGES OF ENGLAND

# PORTSMOUTH AT WAR

ANDREW WHITMARSH

*Frontispiece:* Guardians of Portsmouth. Civil Defence personnel keep a lookout for enemy aircraft, with the Guildhall in the background. (*News* 2009)

First published in 2007 by Tempus Publishing

Reprinted in 2008 by
The History Press
The Mill, Brimscombe Port,
Stroud, Gloucestershire, GL5 2QG
www.thehistorypress.co.uk

Reprinted 2011, 2012

British Library Cataloguing in Publication Data.
A catalogue record for this book is available from the British Library.

ISBN 978 07524 4296 9

Typesetting and origination by
Tempus Publishing Limited.
Printed in Great Britain.

# Contents

# Acknowledgements

The author would like to thank the following: my fiancée Bryony for her support; my employer, Portsmouth City Council, for letting me base the book on the collections of Portsmouth Museums & Records Service; *The News*, Portsmouth, for permission to use wartime photographs from their archives; and the many friends and colleagues who have provided me with assistance and inspiration, both while writing this book and at other times. Finally I wish to thank the hundreds of people who, over the decades since the Second World War, have given photographs, documents and other material relating to the Second World War to Portsmouth Museums & Records Service. Without their generosity, this book would not have been possible. They are too many to acknowledge individually, but I am grateful to them all.

# About the photographs

The photographs and other images used for this book are primarily from the collections of Portsmouth Museums & Records Service (from the Military History and Local History sections, and the Records Office). The Museums & Records Service is part of Portsmouth City Council. The copyright to some of these photographs is held by other organisations or individuals, and the author is grateful to have received permission for their use. The owner of copyright or reproduction rights is indicated in the captions along with the appropriate reference number ('PMRS' for Portsmouth Museums & Records Service, *News* for *The News*, Portsmouth, and 'IWM' for the Imperial War Museum, London).

For enquiries about these photographs, or if you would like to donate photographs or other material (or let us copy it), please contact: Andrew Whitmarsh, Military History Officer, City Museum & Records Office, Museum Road, Portsmouth PO1 2LJ. Tel: 023 9282 7261. Website: www.portsmouthmuseums.co.uk

# Introduction

For centuries, Portsmouth's prosperity was largely based on warfare and the navy which still plays an important part in the city today. The city built, supplied and maintained the royal fleet, and Portsmouth's fortunes rose or declined according to whether England was at peace or at war. For centuries, Portsmouth people have served aboard those ships, or have been part of the army garrison that guarded the city, which was one of Britain's most heavily-defended areas. Yet never did the cost of war hit home as it did during the Second World War. The war was unquestionably Portsmouth's 'Finest Hour'. The city and its people suffered a series of devastating bombing attacks, as well as coping with all the greater or lesser sacrifices and restrictions of wartime. Then in 1944, Portsmouth and the surrounding area played the key role in launching Operation Overlord, the Allied landings in Normandy on D-Day (6 June 1944) and the campaign that followed as the Allies established a foothold in German-occupied Europe.

This book showcases some of the hundreds of photographs taken during the war by Portsmouth people, which have been given to the city's Museums & Records Service over the past six decades. Many of these images have never been seen by the public before. In wartime conditions, the opportunities for photography were limited. Camera film was in short supply for private use, while security considerations and censorship restricted most people's ability to take photographs. Those personal snapshots that were taken typically relate only to family and friends. Another vital source for the book has therefore been the archive of photographs from the city's newspaper, *The News* (then the *Portsmouth Evening News*). These were taken by Victor Stewart, the newspaper's only wartime photographer. Photographs from *The News* have been useful as a record of major events that ordinary people were not able to photograph.

There were two main considerations in choosing images for this book: each had to be a well-composed photograph or a legible document, as well as showing something significant. Not all aspects of Portsmouth's war are recorded in equal numbers of photographs, but every attempt has been made to cover the subject as widely as possible. The collections held by Portsmouth Museums & Records Service mean that this volume focuses on the area within the modern-day boundaries of the city of Portsmouth. Yet Portsmouth's war cannot be considered in complete isolation from its neighbours, such as Gosport and Hayling Island, and where possible other locations have been referred to.

The Second World War brought huge changes to Portsmouth. To take just one simple indicator of change, the city's population fell from over 260,000 before the war to 136,500 in September 1941 (this decrease was due to evacuation, people serving ovrseas, as well as other pressures of war). The experience of war was different for every individual involved: the newly-wed widow who barely got to know her husband before he was killed overseas; the man who fought the fires of the Blitz and then saw active service abroad with the armed forces; the young schoolboy for whom the war was primarily a time of excitement and freedom; the teenage nurse in one of the city's hospitals who treated the civilian casualties of the Blitz as well as the servicemen brought back from the fighting fronts; the housewife who had to see her family through rationing, evacuation and bombing raids; all those who, after a hard day's work (which often contributed to the war effort in some way) then spent their nights on duty as air-raid wardens, fire-watchers or in the Home Guard; the many people who found themselves in previously unknown positions of responsibility and having to make decisions that had major effects for others. This book aims to reflect some of this range of service and experiences.

It is perhaps true that war brings out both the best and the worst in human beings; self-sacrifice and comradeship on the one hand, and cruelty and destruction on the other. Portsmouth in wartime saw countless examples of courage, endurance, community spirit and selflessness. Of course these traits were not universal, and to pretend otherwise – that fear, doubt or self-interest were completely absent – would be a false and romanticised view. Yet the reason for the survival of British society in general, and of Portsmouth's people in particular, was because the vast majority of citizens showed those positive qualities. This book is therefore dedicated not just to all Portsmouth people who were killed or injured during the Second World War, but to all those who lived through it.

# Bibliography

G.E. Barnett (comp.) and V. Blanchard (ed.), *City of Portsmouth. Records of the Corporation 1936-1945*, Corporation of Portsmouth, nd.

Admiral Sir William James, *Portsmouth Letters*, Macmillan & Co., 1946.

Paul Jenkins, *Battle over Portsmouth*, Middleton Press, 1986.

Nigel Peake, *City at War*, Milestone Publications, 1986.

Portsdown Tunnels website, www.portsdown-tunnels.org.uk, 2006.

*Portsmouth Evening News*, Smitten City, nd.

Winston Ramsay (ed.), *The Blitz Then and Now, Vols. 1-2, After the Battle*, 1987-1988.

John Stedman, *Portsmouth Reborn*, Portsmouth City Council, 1995.

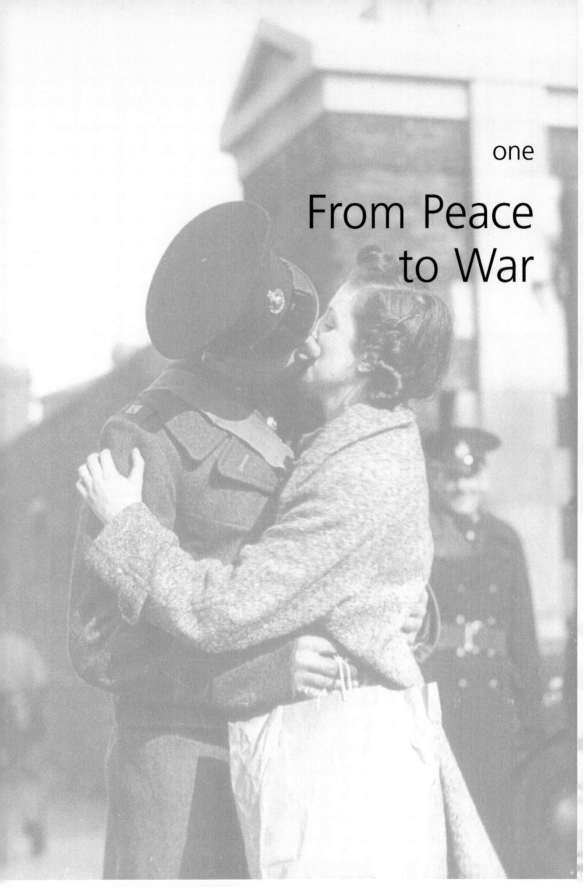

one

# From Peace
# to War

For hundreds of years, Portsmouth had been the foremost naval port of the British Empire. At the end of the 1930s, a new war seemed increasingly likely as Adolf Hitler's Germany repeatedly demanded to expand into further European territories. The city's role as a naval base and its location on the south coast ensured that Portsmouth would be closely involved in the next conflict.

For Britain, the Second World War began on 3 September 1939 with Prime Minister Neville Chamberlain's declaration of war with Germany, following the German invasion of Poland two days earlier. Since the Nazi regime had gained power in Germany in 1933, there had been a series of diplomatic crises, including the announcement in 1935 of German rearmament (forbidden by the treaties signed after the First World War), the absorption of Austria into Germany in 1936, and the German annexation of Czechoslovakia in 1938-1939 (including the Munich Crisis of September 1938). These indications of approaching war gave the British more time to prepare their relatively ill-equipped armed forces and to ready the civilian population for what it was feared would be a sudden and deadly onslaught of bombing raids. The government predicted that on the outbreak of war, air raids would cause 66,000 civilian deaths per week across the nation (in fact, the total number of UK civilians killed by enemy action during the war was 60,595). The government first gave information to local authorities on Air Raid Precautions (ARP) in 1935, and the first air raid wardens were enlisted two years later. ARP preparations in Portsmouth were ridiculed in some quarters until the bombing raids of the Blitz demonstrated their value.

When war came, therefore, it was not a surprise. Many people from the wartime generation remember clustering round the radio (or 'wireless' as it was then known) to hear Chamberlain announce that Britain was now at war with Germany. The experience of the First World War meant that people had some idea of what wartime would be like, but the new conflict was to have much wider effects on the entire civilian population. Precautions were put into action straight away, with the issuing of Anderson Shelters (air raid shelters) and gas masks. Since Portsmouth was judged to be a likely target for enemy aircraft, many local children were evacuated to what were considered to be safer places. Before long, rationing of food and clothing was introduced. Families and friends were split apart as men and women went away to join the armed forces or other wartime services. Sometimes loved ones serving overseas would not be seen again for many years – or in the case of those who were killed in the fighting, never again. Yet everyday life still went on. People still went to work and enjoyed their leisure time (although there was much less of the latter than before), fell in love and got married, raised families and grew up. However the war and its effects were always present.

*Right:* Brigadier Bernard Montgomery in 1938 when he was Portsmouth Garrison commander. He is outside his residence, Ravelin House, now part of Portsmouth University. Before long he would be famous as 'Monty', commander of the Eighth Army in North Africa and Italy, and Allied ground forces commander in the 1944 Normandy Landings. With him are his son David (right) and the son of another Army officer. (PMRS 1987/501/1)

*Below:* Members of the British Union of Fascists (the Blackshirts) on parade in Southsea in around 1936. They are emerging onto South Parade from Burgoyne Road, Southsea. On one occasion the leader of this fascist party, Oswald Mosley, visited the city and held a rally at the Guildhall, but was greeted by large crowds voicing their opposition. (PMRS 2003/2739)

In about 1936, the council's central depot fitted this Dennis street-cleaning lorry with spray nozzles on the front and sides, as a way of dealing with poison gas dropped by enemy aircraft. Fortunately this equipment was never needed. (PMRS 1945/652/8)

The Police control room at Portsmouth during an ARP exercise in March 1938. Imaginary 'incidents' (as locations where bombs had fallen were known) have been plotted on a wall map. The city was blacked out and over 1,000 ARP personnel dealt with a simulated air raid. This was the same month that the German annexation of Austria took place, heightening the fear of war. (*News*)

PC Jack Hancock (left) and PC Goronwy Wynne Evans outside Portsmouth Guildhall, not long before the outbreak of war. Sandbags were put up around the entrance to the building in September 1938 as protection against bombing. This was a response to the Munich Crisis. PC Evans won the George Medal for fire fighting on 10-11 January 1941. (PMRS 1994/593)

Testing a barrage balloon on Southsea Common in 1938. The event has drawn quite a crowd. The amusement arcades of Clarence Pier can be seen in the background, but war clouds were already beginning to overshadow the otherwise peaceful scene. (PMRS 1990/35/11)

*Above:* Anti-aircraft guns on Southsea Common not long before the outbreak of war. These are 3-inch guns (this refers to the diameter of the shells they fired). Shortages of modern weapons meant that older equipment such as these First World War-era guns had to be used at first. The soldiers' tents and the Queen's Hotel can be seen in the background. (*News*)

*Left:* Mrs F. Clarke preparing sandbags to protect her house. The windows have been covered with sticky tape to prevent flying fragments of glass if they were broken by bomb blast. (PMRS 1122A/1/2/2)

**URGENT NOTICE.**

CITY OF PORTSMOUTH.

# VOLUNTEERS

ARE VERY URGENTLY

# REQUIRED

## FOR FILLING SANDBAGS

### AT ONCE.

Volunteers should bring their own spade or shovel if possible **and Report to the City Engineer, The Guildhall, Portsmouth.**

The Guildhall, Portsmouth. August, 1939.

LEONARD N. BLAKE, Lord Mayor.

In the last days of peace, this poster appealed for local people to help fill sandbags in order to protect public buildings or air-raid shelters. The same appeal was also made in *The Evening News* on 2 September 1939. Communal shelters reinforced with sand bags were sometimes built in the streets for use by local residents. These were different from public shelters, which were for members of the public who were away from their home or workplace at the time of an air raid. (PMRS 2005/525)

Ivy Tibbles (later Ivy Anthony), facing camera was one of those who answered the appeal to fill sandbags, and is seen here at work on Eastney beach. Many people feared that the war would begin with a series of bombing raids that would cause horrific casualties. In the event it was to be more than ten months before the first bombs fell on the city. (PMRS 2002/601)

*Above:* Mrs Houghton and her daughter Joan construct their Anderson Shelter in their back garden at St Mary's Road, Fratton, in late 1939. By October 1940, there were 24,000 Anderson Shelters in Portsmouth, as well as 2,200 brick shelters, 800 strengthened basements, communal shelters with a capacity for 5,000 people, plus public shelters. Other people sheltered under the stairs of their houses. (PMRS 1992/595/4)

*Left:* Iris Voss (later Iris Comben) in June 1941 outside the Anderson Shelter in the garden of her home in Cumberland Road, Southsea. For additional comfort, the family have fitted their shelter with an old cupboard door. At the height of the bombing raids many families regularly spent the whole night in their Anderson Shelter. (PMRS 1993/508)

*Above:* A group of children practice wearing their gas masks, in Clacton Road, Wymering. Most wear the standard civilian gas mask. Children under five years old have the 'Mickey Mouse' version, which was brightly coloured and had twin eye holes. Since gas was not used, after a while most people gave up carrying their gas masks. (*News*)

*Right:* A member of the Air Raid Precautions staff demonstrates the use of a baby's 'gas helmet' at All Saints church, Portsea. In the event of a gas attack, the concertina apparatus on the side had to be continually pumped up and down to force air through the filter. Both the baby and its mother look unconvinced! (*News* 95)

Policemen supervise as evacuees and their teachers board buses at Greetham Street, next to Portsmouth and Southsea train station, in the first two days of September 1939. Less than half the city's 28,000 schoolchildren chose to be evacuated, along with mothers with young children, and blind people. They went to places such as Salisbury, Winchester or the New Forest. (*News* 1)

Evacuees from Frances Avenue School in Southsea (foreground), aged between eight and nine, share a classroom with local children at a Ventnor school in 1939-1940. Over 3,000 Portsmouth evacuees went to the Isle of Wight in September 1939. In the absence of bombing raids, many evacuees returned to Portsmouth by Christmas 1939. (*News*)

*Above:* Children from Langstone School board a train at Portsmouth and Southsea station on 28 June 1940. Three days earlier, the German invasion of France had ended with the final surrender of French forces. The renewed threat of attack on the UK led to this second wave of evacuations. Most of this school's children were not evacuated, but those that did go mainly went to the Winchester area. (*News* 906)

*Right:* In 1939, Jeanne Niblett was evacuated to the Isle of Wight, but soon returned to her family home in Kimberley Road, Southsea. Here, in mid-1940 when Jeanne was aged ten, she waits for the bus that will take her to stay with relatives in Wiltshire, where she lived for over three years. (PMRS 2002/621)

A class of boys and their teacher display trophies collected from the streets of Portsmouth, including bullets and fragments of bomb casings. For children, life in wartime could be exciting as often as it was frightening or sad. (*News* 1122)

A class of girls at Stamshaw School in 1942. All Portsmouth schools were closed after the evacuations of June 1940 but many reopened over the next six months because so many children were still left in the city. (PMRS 1994/499)

*Above:* Over 100 volunteers prepared 260,000 ration books and coupons for Portsmouth residents at the Northern Secondary School in October 1939. Food rationing did not come into force until 8 January 1940, initially only for sugar, bacon, ham and butter. (*News* 208A)

*Below:* Women queuing outside Portsmouth Guildhall to apply for air-raid shelters. The lady carrying the wicker basket was Mrs Lucy Slater of Chatsworth Avenue, Cosham. She successfully applied for a brick shelter in her garden. Her sister, who lived with her, was in a wheelchair and could not easily get through the narrow doorway of the standard Anderson Shelter. (*News* 923)

# NOTICE.

## THIS RESTAURANT
will be Closed at **10.30**
P.M.

### Late Evening
Customers are served <u>only</u>
on the understanding that
<u>Payment is made at time
of Serving,</u> and that they
**MUST LEAVE on sounding
of the Siren.**

This allows Staff and
ourselves to take cover.

## PUBLIC SHELTERS
## IN VICINITY.

*Left:* Wartime conditions meant that new rules had to be introduced for everyday situations. Restaurant staff had to ensure that customers would not leave to take shelter during an air raid without having paid for their meals! This notice was put up in the Continental Café in Commercial Road. Run by Mr B.E. Albertolli, the café was closed for only five days during the war. (PMRS 972A)

*Below:* The interior of one of Portsmouth's British Restaurants, also known as Municipal Restaurants. These were set up across the city to provide good but cheap food for which a ration book was not required. The one on Lake Road could seat 500 people and was the largest on the south coast. (*News* 1700)

Army Form E.518

## RESERVE AND AUXILIARY FORCES ACT, 1939.
## TERRITORIAL ARMY.

### CALLING OUT NOTICE.

To—

Name ......................... *Kinch   G.H.*

Rank ......................... *Gr.* ......................... Army Number *1428711*

Regt. or Corps ......... *214/57th·Wessex·A.A.Regt...R.A.T.*

In pursuance of directions given by the Secretary of State for War in accordance with an Order in Council made under Section 1 of the above-mentioned Act, you are hereby notified that you are called out for military service commencing from *20 AUG 1939* 19 , and for this purpose you are required to join the *214th·Southsea·A.A.Ety.R.A.T,*     **St Paul's Road**

at..........*Time to be notified later*.....on that day.

Should you not present yourself on that day you will be liable to be proceeded against.

*R.H.Willis*

**MAJOR, R.A**
**COMDG. 214th (SOUTHSEA) A.A. BATTERY, R.A**
*Stamp of Officer Commanding Unit.*

Place......... **Portsmouth.**

Date .............*7*....*JUL*...*1939*..................

You should bring your Health and Pensions Insurance Card and Unemployment Insurance Book. If, however, you cannot obtain these before joining you should write to your employer asking him to forward these to you at your unit headquarters. If you are in possession of a receipt (U.I. 40) from the Employment Exchange for your Employment Book bring that receipt with you.

You will also bring your Army Book 3, but you *must not fill* in any particulars on page 13 or the " Statement of family " in that book, and the postcards therein *must not be used.*

(303/2242) Wt. 14343—678  -OM  5/39  H & S Ltd.  Gp. 393  Forms E518/1

As war approached, the part-time soldiers of the Territorial Army were warned that they would be called up. This notice was sent to Gordon Kinch of 214th Battery, part of 57th Heavy Anti-Aircraft Regiment. The battery was raised in Southsea, with the regiment's other three batteries (213th, 215th and 219th) being formed of men from Portsmouth, Gosport and the Isle of Wight. (PMRS 2003/1732)

Local women join the Auxiliary Territorial Service (ATS), the British Army's service for women. ATS women performed a huge range of tasks, including serving as cooks, drivers, military police and intelligence analysts. At its greatest size, the ATS numbered around 250,000 women, making it the largest of the three women's services. (*News*)

*Above:* Children could also 'join up'. Here, King George VI inspects naval cadets in Guildhall Square during his visit on 30 September 1942. To the right of the King is Admiral Sir William James, commander-in-chief of Portsmouth Naval Command, and at far left is the Lord Mayor, Sir Denis Daley. (*News*)

*Left:* A Royal Marine kissing goodbye to his wife or girlfriend outside the Royal Marine barracks at Eastney in 1939. For those serving abroad, particularly in the Middle East or Far East, it could be years before they were able to return to the UK on leave. (*News* 197)

*Right:* An airgraph message sent to Chief Petty Officer Ralph Thorpe at Christmas 1944 by former colleagues at *The Evening News*, Portsmouth. This paper message was photographed, then the negative was sent by air and was photographically reprinted at the other end. This removed the need to transport bulky mail bags. Thorpe was awarded the British Empire Medal for his wartime service with submarines, and was played by Sid James in the 1958 film *The Silent Enemy*. (PMRS 2005/893)

*Below:* George Drain of the Royal Navy sent this recorded voice message to his father at Arnaud Street, Buckland. With a centuries-old tradition of navy and army service, Portsmouth people were no strangers to loved ones being absent for long periods overseas. That did not necessarily make it any easier to bear however. (PMRS 2003/1669)

Portsmouth women packing care packages for British prisoners of war held in enemy countries. Prisoners of war were sometimes poorly treated and were often short of food. Care packages were therefore important. (*News*)

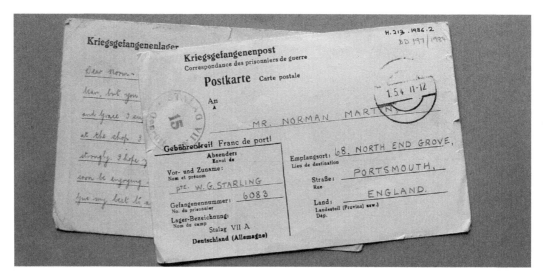

Postcards sent by Private Bill Starling in 1942 and 1944 to his friend Norman Martin of North End Grove. Prisoners of war often faced years of hardship and boredom before being set free. Postcards like these were a rare opportunity to communicate with family and friends, even though the mail would have been censored by their captors. (PMRS 1986/213/1-2)

*Above:* The wedding of Jim and Norah Parsons in Milton, November 1945. He served with No. 9 Squadron RAF, and she worked at Airspeed. Rationing of clothing and food meant that wartime weddings were often fairly simple. In many cases, the new husband and wife were separated not long after they were married, when the man went to serve overseas. (PMRS EF1743)

*Right:* A worried crowd gathers at the Royal Naval Barracks to read a list of men killed on board HMS *Royal Oak* on the night of 13-14 October 1939. The battleship was sunk with the loss of 833 lives by the German submarine U-47 at the Scapa Flow naval base in the Orkneys. It was perhaps this tragedy that that the Lord Mayor, Denis Daley, was thinking of when he said later that year, 'We in Portsmouth know quite well what war means. Indeed, there are very few cities and towns in the country to which war has a deeper meaning.' (*News* 174)

1942

Aug
Fri 28 Song of The Islands — Betty Grable ODEON
Color — Vic Mature Jack Oakie
Sabotage at Sea — Jane Carr.
Sept
Sat 5 Unpublished Story — Richard Greene SAVOY
Valerie Hobson
GERT & Dais Clean Up. — Elsie & Doris Waters.
Sat 12 FIRST OF THE FEW — Leslie Howard ODEON
David Niven
Oct
Tues 6 Holiday Inn — Bing Crosby ODEON
Fred Astaire
Sun 11 Son of Fury — Tyrone Power G. Sanders PLAZA
MAN Who Returned to Life — John Howard.
Sat 17 GONE WITH THE WIND. — Clark Gable Viv. Leigh SAVOY
COLOR — Leslie Howard Olivia de Havilland
Called up Oct 23rd 1942.

*Above:* A list kept by Dulcie Childs of Kimbolton Road, Copnor, showing films that she saw in 1942, including the famous *Gone With the Wind*. A week after the last entry, she was called up into the ATS, and subsequently served as a clerk with the Royal Army Pay Corps. (PMRS 2004/3517)

*Left:* The cover of a booklet promoting 'Holidays at Home' in the Portsmouth area. Wartime conditions, such as security restrictions and petrol rationing, made travel difficult for most people. The public were encouraged to spend their leisure time near where they lived. Even holidays could contribute to the war effort; the guide states that wartime experience 'has shown that with long working hours our health and efficiency are impaired and production suffers, unless we have relaxation.' (PMRS 2005/545)

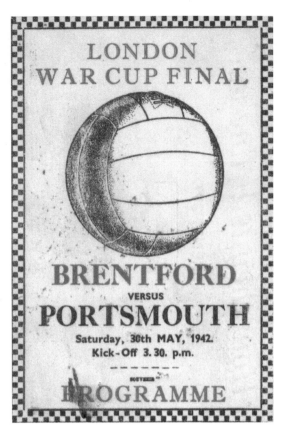

On 29 April 1939, Portsmouth Football Club won the FA cup by beating Wolves 4-1. Seven members of that team took part in this game at Wembley against Brentford on 30 May 1942 (Pompey lost 2-0). League football was suspended for the war years. Pompey played friendly matches in 'war leagues' using players who had not yet been called up, as well as other servicemen based in the city. (PMRS 1256A/1)

Part of the programme for The King's Theatre, Southsea, in late June 1944. Theatres, cinemas and football grounds were all closed on the outbreak of war, but this decision was reversed two weeks later. (PMRS 1131A/8/3)

---

**Week commencing Monday, June 26th, 1944**
**Nightly at 6.30.**
**Matinees Thurs. & Sat., 2.30**
BERNARD DELFONT presents

# VAUDEVILLE OF 1944.

1—THE KINGS THEATRE ORCHESTRA
             Under the direction of CHAS. H. PETERS

2—VIC RAY & LUCILLE    ...    Your own Dancing Stars

3—DUDLEY DALE   ...     ...      Unique

4—LEWIS KING    ...   The Golden Voice of Radio

5—READING & GRANTLEY     Fun on the Trampoline

6—KUDA BUX   ...    ...   The Man with X-Ray Eyes

INTERVAL

The Bars of the Theatre are fully licensed. Matinee Teas can be obtained from the Attendants or at the Bars.

7—VIC RAY & LUCILLE       In a welcome re-appearance

8—DUDLEY DALE introduces JOYCE MAXWELL
                          Music and Glamour

9—MURRAY & MOONEY    ...    The famous Radio Stars

10—LAMONTE & JULIE TRIO
              With Hand-Balancing and Juggling

Military policemen check a cyclist's identity documents in Festing Road, Southsea, on 17 August 1943. An emergency water pipe can be seen next to the pavement on the right. These pipes were laid as a backup system, after so many of the normal water mains were cut by high explosive bombs during the air raid of 10 January 1941, making it very difficult to extinguish fires from incendiary bombs. (*News*)

Earlier in the war, in July 1940, a German invasion seemed likely and security restrictions were introduced in the seafront area. South Parade Pier and Clarence Pier were closed. The restrictions were relaxed slightly over time, and bathing was subsequently permitted on the beach between Southsea Castle and Clarence Pier in the early evenings.

From noon on 17 August 1943 onwards, however, only people bearing a special permit were allowed to enter the Southsea seafront area. This permit was in addition to the normal identity card that everyone had to carry in wartime. Permits were only given to residents and to people who had another legitimate reason to enter the area. On 1 April 1944, as D-Day drew nearer, similar security restrictions were imposed throughout a zone ten miles deep along the south and east coasts of England.

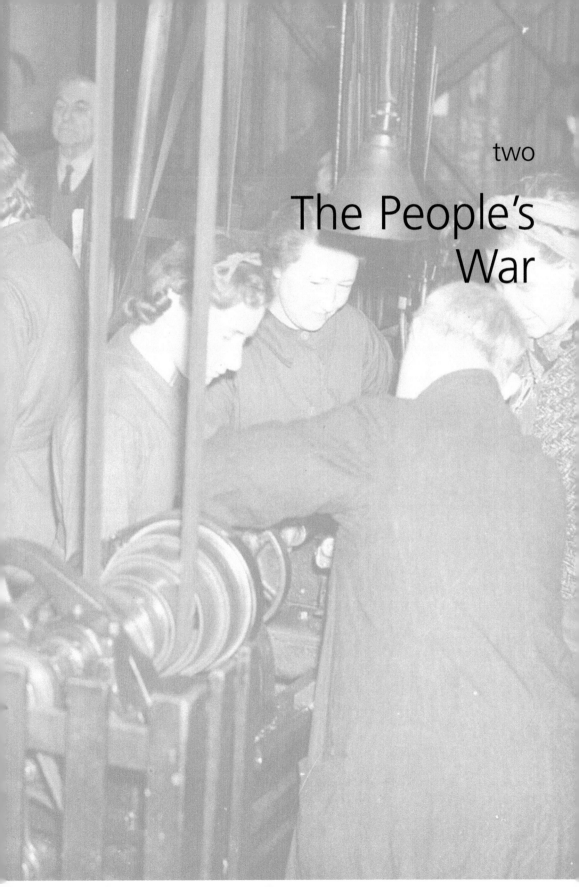

two

# The People's War

The Second World War was a 'total war' in a way that no previous conflict had been. Civilians were almost as likely to be killed or injured as service personnel. At the same time, all members of society were called upon to support the war effort in some way. Those who could not join the armed forces could work in an armaments factory, collect scrap metal that could be used in weapons production, or help raise money to pay for the war. Men, women and children, the young and old, were all encouraged to play a part in the war in some way. Often these efforts were organised by the city council and led by the lord mayor or lady mayoress. Other campaigns were organised by groups such as the Women's Voluntary Service (renamed the Women's Royal Voluntary Service after the war), the Women's Institute, the Scouts and others. Since the whole cross-section of the population was involved, the home front in the Second World War is sometimes known as the People's War.

Food rationing was introduced in January 1940, and clothes rationing in June 1941. Rationing and other wartime restrictions gave people personal as well as patriotic incentives to fight the battles on the Home Front – or in the words of wartime government slogans, to 'Dig for Victory' and 'Lend a hand on the land' (increasing food production), 'Make do and mend' (re-using scrap materials, especially for clothes) and 'Lend to defend the right to be free' or 'Hit back with National Savings' (fund-raising or lending money to the government).

When it came to employment, working towards the war effort was compulsory for some people, although many men and women volunteered for war service. Men aged eighteen to forty-one (extended to fifty-one in December 1941) were conscripted into the armed services, unless they were in a 'reserved occupation' (such as certain dockyard work) in which they were judged to be too valuable to the war effort to be called up. Women played a vital role in working for the war effort. From 1941, women could also be conscripted into war industries, the women's branches of the armed forces or Civil Defence (as ARP was known after that year). In the chemicals and explosives industries – vital in the manufacture of munitions – 52 per cent of factory workers were female, for example. In addition, over a million people aged over sixty-five were also in employment. This was sometimes referred to as the 'industrial army', which worked in tandem with the fighting army overseas. Many people – both men and women – who did a long day's work during the day would often do other war work at night, in services such as the Home Guard or Civil Defence. These long hours sometimes left a legacy of post-war ill-health that was never recognised by the state.

*Opposite above:* A group of older men, no doubt including First World War veterans, work on the allotments at Baffins early in the war. Food grown in allotments and gardens helped reduce the amount that had to be imported from overseas. (*News* 78)

*Opposite below:* Members of the Women's Voluntary Service (WVS) collect aluminium pots and kettles for the war effort, perhaps to be made into aircraft parts. They are in Guildhall Square, next to the statue of Queen Victoria (since moved to a new position). By the end of August 1940, Portsmouth had collected over eight and a half tons of scrap metal. (*News* 947)

Members of the first aid party of No. 1 ARP (Air Raid Precautions) Depot from Milton organise a scrap-collecting party for the war effort, December 1941. Their wagon bears signs reading 'We have no petrol but plenty of spirit' and 'Save the scrap to scrap the rat'. The slogans were created by one of the ARP staff. (*News* 1950)

Lord Mayor Sir Denis Daley opens 'Salvage Week' on 19 January 1942. The phrase 'a scrap of paper' was the way Adolf Hitler subsequently described the Anglo-German agreement signed at Munich in September 1938; he did not wait long before breaking it. (*News*)

Assisted by scouts and other youth groups, the lord mayor collects books in Highland Road, Southsea, on 26 July 1942. The books were sold to raise money for Portsmouth hospitals. Books were also collected for the armed forces or for bombed-out public libraries. (*News*)

The finale of a Combined Services Tattoo on 19 August 1944, held at Fratton Park football ground. A large audience watched parades and displays by the Royal Marines, Home Guard, Civil Defence and Fire Services, youth groups and others. Such displays promoted the work done by these groups and encouraged support for the war effort. (PMRS 2004/3904)

A huge crowd of Portsmouth people of all ages gathered in Guildhall Square for a national day of prayer on 26 May 1940. Lord Mayor Denis Daley (wearing his chain of office) can be seen speaking near the centre of the photograph. On the left, wearing a formal wig, is the Town Clerk and ARP Controller, Frederick Sparks. That same day, British troops began to be evacuated from Dunkirk and other French ports, in the face of the German invasion of France. By 3 June, around 338,000 Allied soldiers had been brought back to the UK, more than anticipated. Many came back to Portsmouth. (*News*)

A parade in Guildhall Square on 20 March 1942 to open the Warship Week fundraising campaign. Passing the Sussex Hotel are members of the WVS who cared for people made homeless in the Blitz. During this week, Portsmouth raised nearly £1.3 million to pay for the cruiser HMS *Sirius*. Parades to promote fundraising campaigns were a regular feature of wartime Portsmouth. (*News*)

A Fairey Fulmar fighter aircraft of the Royal Navy's Fleet Air Arm on display in Guildhall Square on 31 May 1943 as part of Wings for Victory Week. The city eventually raised just under £1.2 million in this campaign, enough to pay for around 100 Spitfire fighters. (*News*)

*Above:* A board showing the money raised by the Savings Group at Hilltop Crescent, Widley, during Salute the Soldier Week in 1942. After the war, the government paid back money invested in War Savings, plus interest. Savings groups were organised by housewives, pensioners and even schoolchildren. (PMRS 1985/50/3)

*Right:* Women took over the traditionally male role of postman. Before the war, a woman who worked was sometimes seen as taking a job away from a man who needed it, and in some jobs women had to resign after they got married. During the war, however, war work even became compulsory for many women. (*News*)

*Above:* Female engineering apprentices being trained in their new work. Women taking on skilled work that had previously only been done by men were given the unflattering name of 'dilutees'. They were given a short course in just one part of the job, rather than an apprentice's full training. (*News*)

*Left:* In June 1940, the first women bus conductors were introduced in the city, and by the end of 1941 there were 120 of them. A further step was taken by Mrs E.V. Hunt and Mrs K.E. Devine of Portsmouth, seen here, who in 1941 became the first two women in England to qualify to drive a double-decker bus. (*News*)

Dockyard workers watch as Portsmouth's Lady Mayoress, Lady Margaret Daley, prepares to launch Admiralty Floating Dock No. 21 on 9 March 1943. During the war, the number of dockyard workers peaked at 25,000, of whom 3,000 were women. The men were in reserved occupations, considered so vital to the war effort that they could not be called up into the armed forces. (*News* 2497)

Admiralty Floating Dock No. 21 is launched at Portsmouth Dockyard on 9 March 1943. Some dockyard departments were moved out of the city to escape the bombing, but throughout the war the dockyard continued to play a vital role in repairing, refitting and modifying ships. (*News* 2502)

Two women working on a motor torpedo boat (MTB) at Vosper's yard. These small, fast, torpedo-armed craft fought regular skirmishes with the German navy in the English Channel. Vosper's original boatyard at Broad Street, Old Portsmouth, was destroyed by German air raids in early 1941, but the company had already opened a new yard at Portchester. (1990/1318/15, courtesy of VT Group)

The wingless fuselage of an Oxford aircraft at the Airspeed company's factory at Portsmouth airport, in Hilsea. Nearly half of the total number of Oxfords built during the war – 4,411 – were built here. The twin-engine Oxford played a vital part in training the pilots, bomb-aimers, navigators, radio operators and air gunners of the Royal Air Force's bomber squadrons. (PMRS 1989/156)

Members of the Women's Land Army train with tractors at Hambledon Down, north of Portsmouth, in October 1939. Land Army women replaced male farm workers who had joined the armed forces. It was important to increase food production so that Britain would not be starved into surrender by the German U-boat (submarine) blockade. (*News*)

The 1.3 million women of the Women's Voluntary Service (WVS) produced many of the camouflage nets required for covering up military equipment. These WVS ladies are at Emsworth. They wove strips of material into the netting to create irregular patterns. Other groups such as the Women's Institute also made significant voluntary contributions to the war effort. (*News*)

WVS staff at Hilsea Services Club are visited by the Lord Mayor and Lady Mayoress of Portsmouth, Denis and Margaret Daley, on 15 November 1940. To their right is the Chief Constable, Arthur Charles West. These clubs aimed to provide a home from home for servicemen, with cooked meals, games, a reading room and so on. (*News*)

Members of the Hampshire 11 Detachment of the British Red Cross in the grounds of what is now Priory School, at Fawcett Road, Southsea, in around 1942. Members of the Red Cross and the St John Ambulance Brigade played a vital part in the ARP casualty services, treating the wounded before they reached hospital. (PMRS 1994/346)

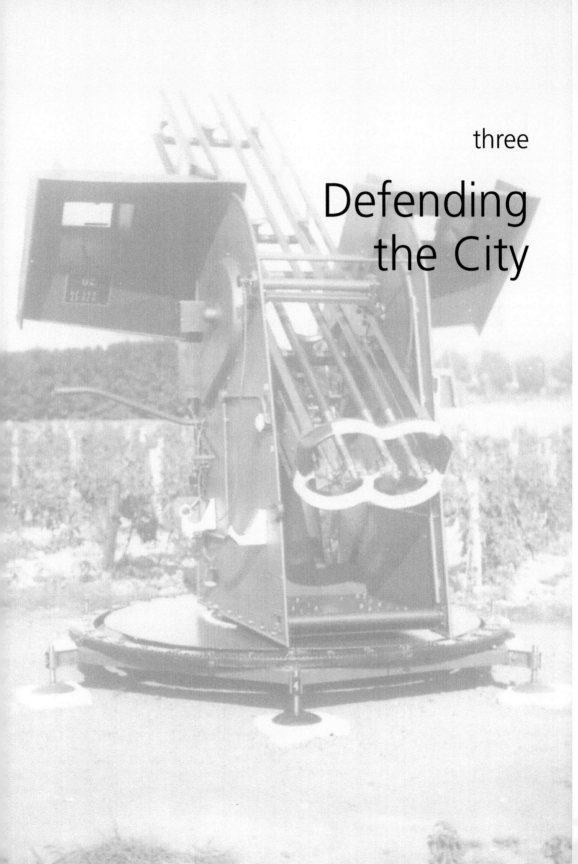

three

Defending
the City

During the Second World War, any city in the United Kingdom could potentially come under enemy attack, but Portsmouth was particularly under threat. Its importance to the Royal Navy – due to the dockyard and the other naval bases in the area – made it a valuable target for air raids. The city's location on the south coast also meant that it was regularly over-flown by enemy aircraft as they headed for other targets further inland. Each time aircraft approached, the air-raid alarms were sounded and the defences were put on alert. Defending the city and protecting its inhabitants required the services of a huge number of people in a variety of roles. Some were members of the armed forces or were otherwise employed on a full-time basis, but many were local people serving in a part-time, voluntary role.

For the first eight months of the war, air attack was the main threat to Portsmouth, and the city had heavy defences. The city and the surrounding area was guarded by anti-aircraft guns (manned for the first years of the war by local men of the Territorial Army), barrage balloons and searchlights. They defended the city during the attacks of the Battle of Britain and the Blitz in 1940-1941. To deal with the aftermath of air raids, the Air Raid Precautions (ARP) service was created before the war, and from 1941 was known instead as Civil Defence. During summer 1940, local residents formed Neighbourhood Supplementary Fire Parties. Theoretically intended only to deal with the aftermath of raids, many of these groups also tackled fires while bombing was still taking place. They were later replaced with the nationally organised Fire Guard.

In July 1940, after the defeat of France, Adolf Hitler ordered that preparations be made for the invasion of Britain. The Home Guard had been set up two months previously, ready for just such an eventuality. Fear of invasion reached its peak that September. Historians now debate whether the Germans really intended to invade, or whether Hitler simply hoped that his preparations would persuade the British to make peace. Under the German plans for the invasion – Operation Sealion – the initial landings would have taken place in Kent rather than near the Solent, but the Home Guard did not know that at the time. As the invasion threat subsided, the Home Guard also began to play an increasing role in anti-aircraft and coastal defence.

To a large extent, Portsmouth and its residents were defended and aided by local people, giving up their time and often placing themselves in positions of greater danger in order to try to protect their friends and neighbours. Great assistance was of course provided by armed forces personnel from outside the area, and also by organisations or individuals from further abroad – such as the Canadian firemen who were based in the city from 1942 to 1944.

As this German photograph taken in August 1940 shows, the Luftwaffe (German air force) was well aware of the many potential targets in the Portsmouth area. They included the dockyard, Vosper's ship-building workshops in Old Portsmouth, the submarine base of HMS *Dolphin* in Gosport, as well as local railway lines and barracks. (PMRS 694A/10/1)

The Battle of Britain lasted from mid-June to mid-September 1940. Its purpose was to prepare the way for a German invasion of Britain by destroying the Royal Air Force (RAF), an aim that was fortunately never achieved. The Blitz is the name given to the Luftwaffe's campaign of night attacks on British cities from August 1940 to May 1941. It began during the Battle of Britain, partly as an attempt to destroy aircraft factories and thereby reduce the number of fighter planes available to the RAF. By the end, the Blitz was simply an attempt to force the British people and government to surrender due to the death and destruction being inflicted.

In addition to the defences around Portsmouth, air raids on the city were also met by fighter aircraft from nearby airfields, such as Tangmere. The radar station at Ventnor on the Isle of Wight provided early warning as enemy bombers approached. Once the German aircraft were over land, and inside the line of radar stations (which faced out to sea), the men and women of the Royal Observer Corps reported on their movements.

The Portsmouth area's anti-aircraft defences stretched from Gosport to Hayling Island. The 4.5-inch anti-aircraft gun – such as this one on Southsea Common – could fire eight rounds per minute, to a height of 34,500ft (6.5 miles or 10km). The gun shield provided limited protection for the crew, who had to remain at their posts as the bombs fell around them. During the air raid of 10 March 1941, the Southsea Common gun site was hit by two bombs, killing eleven men of 215th Battery, 57th Heavy Anti-Aircraft Regiment. On 17 April 1941, more than thirty German bombs were dropped near the 4.5-inch guns at Sinah, Hayling Island, killing six men of the same regiment's 219th Battery and wounding thirty. (*News* 2744)

*Right:* Two women of the Auxiliary Territorial Service (ATS) using an identification telescope at a local anti-aircraft gun site. A 3.7-inch anti-aircraft gun can be seen in the background. Mixed anti-aircraft batteries, in which more than half the personnel were women, were introduced towards the end of 1941. The female crews were not officially permitted to actually fire the guns. (*News*)

*Below:* A battery of 3.7-inch anti-aircraft guns in 1940, north-west of Fort Southwick. They had a maximum rate of fire of ten rounds per minute, firing shells to a height of 32,000ft (6 miles, or nearly 10km). This was one of three batteries positioned in case German aircraft approached Portsmouth from inland. (*News* 304)

A barrage balloon in Portsmouth in April 1942, behind the seafront fortifications near King's Bastion. The crew are from the Women's Auxiliary Air Force (WAAF), which was founded in June 1939. There were eventually just over 180,000 women serving in the WAAF, in roles such as office staff, drivers, mechanics and radar operators. (*News* 2025)

Barrage balloons flying over Portsmouth in September 1943, with the ruins of St Paul's church and the Guildhall in the background. This watercolour was painted by local man Albert White while he was on leave from the Army. Each balloon supported a steel cable. Enemy aircraft had to fly higher to avoid the cables, and as a result dropped their bombs less accurately. (PMRS 1999/674)

*Right:* Another anti-aircraft weapon based at Alexandra Park and on Southsea Common was the 3-inch rocket projector, units of which were known as a Z Battery. They fired large numbers of rockets simultaneously, creating a mass of explosions in the sky. This projector at Alexandra Park was manned by 102nd Anti-Aircraft Battery, commanded by Major R.H. Beaver. In the background are some of the unit's award-winning allotments, which were visited by BBC radio's gardening expert, Mr G.H. Middleton, who championed the 'Dig for Victory' campaign. (PMRS 2004/3992)

*Below:* From 1942, some rocket batteries were manned by the Home Guard. These men of 101st Rocket Company, Hampshire Home Guard, are having a meal at their mess at the Gladstone Hotel, Clarence Parade, Southsea. Among them are Sergeant Ken Dean (seated, far end of left-hand row) and Regimental Sergeant Major Gaiger (far right). (PMRS 2005/548)

Sailors set up a machine gun in March 1942 on Unicorn Road, near the Royal Naval Barracks. In the event of a German invasion, Portsea Island would have been defended by the Royal Navy, Royal Marines, Home Guard and Army. The white bands on the trees in the background were painted on to aid drivers in the blackout. (*News* 2017)

Members of the Dockyard Defence Volunteers (as the Dockyard Home Guard was initially known) being inspected by the King in July 1940. The unit was later renamed the 18th Battalion, Hampshire Home Guard. (*News* 982)

Home Guard men under training at the City of Portsmouth Passenger Transport Depot at Methuen Road, Eastney. Most have no military uniform apart from an armband, but their expressions show that this is no *Dad's Army* comedy. By 30 May 1940, 1,500 Portsmouth men had joined the Home Guard. (*News* 1306)

One of a series of instructional drawings produced by Sergeant Charlie Ring for the 17th (Portsmouth) Battalion of the Hampshire Home Guard. He was a painter in the dockyard for more than thirty years, and for a time he drew the 'Dinghy Dan' cartoon for *The Evening News*. (PMRS 2005/1263)

*Above:* A Home Guard band marches along Grand Parade, Old Portsmouth, in early 1941. Ten band members were First World War veterans, and the drum major had served in the Boer War of 1899-1902! In addition to their normal Home Guard duties, the band put on concerts for people 'holidaying at home'. (PMRS 2005/1014)

*Above:* A group of Southsea ARP (Air Raid Precautions) wardens, 1939-1940. Wardens' roles included giving advice to the public, ensuring that the blackout was enforced, and reporting the fall of bombs. In November 1940 there were 560 wardens in paid positions in Portsmouth, as well as over 1,200 part-time volunteer wardens. (PMRS 1996/660)

*Right:* ARP warden Mrs Mitchard outside the warden's post in the basement of the barber shop that she ran with her husband in Jessie Road, Southsea. The photograph was taken by Thomas Price, another one of the wardens there. There were usually six wardens per post (not all of whom would be on duty at once), and one post per 500 inhabitants. (PMRS 1998/472)

*Opposite below:* The White and Newton Company of the 17th (Portsmouth) Battalion, Hampshire Home Guard, take part in a demonstration near HMS *Vernon*, Portsmouth. Their 2lb anti-tank gun was considered obsolete by the Army. White and Newton was a furniture manufacturer that switched over to wartime production of parts for wooden Airspeed Horsa gliders. (PMRS 2005/1055)

ARP personnel at the Royal Hospital, Commercial Road, practice with their gas masks. The rear of the lorry behind them is filled with a non-lethal gas and is sealed with blankets so that they could test how well their masks fitted. The hospital was badly damaged in the air raid of 10 January 1941. (PMRS 1967M/87/9)

FORM "A"

## CITY OF PORTSMOUTH
### Air Raid Wardens' Service.

## CHECK OF CIVILIAN RESPIRATORS

Group: ........................   Post No: _K 6_

Road or Street: _Langley R°_   Date: _May 4" 40_

| Number of House | Surname | Christian Names | L | M | S | Special Childs' | Babies' Helmets | Not examined Inspection form given |
|---|---|---|---|---|---|---|---|---|
| 1 | Barber | Alice | | 1 | | | | ⌐ |
| 3 | DUCK | Audrey | | 1 | | | | |
| " | " | Dorothy | | 1 | | | | |
| 5 | JOLLIEFE | Emily | | 1 | | | | |
| " | " | Andrew | 1 | | | | 1 | |
| 7 | BEARDSHAW | Alice | | 1 | | | | |
| " | " | Derrick | | | 1 | | 1 | |
| 9 | WEBB | Charles | 1 | | | | | |
| 11 | CANFIELD | Eliza | | 1 | | | | |
| " | " | George | 1 | | | | | |
| 13 | WADE | Emily | | 1 | | | | |
| " | " | Edith | | 1 | | | | |
| " | " | Derrick | | | | | 1 | |
| " | ANSTEED | William | | 1 | | | | |

A form used by air-raid wardens in one of their regular duties: checking that gas masks fitted well and were still in good condition. In this case, the form was completed for Langley Road, Buckland, on 4 May 1940. It lists all individuals at each of the properties and the type of respirator (as they were officially known) issued to each. (PMRS 2003/1601)

Men and women of First Aid Post & Depot No. 5 at Kent Street Infants' School, Portsea, in September 1939. The letters 'FAP' on their helmets indicate their role. At the outbreak of war there were eighty-four first aid parties spread across twenty depots, Many of their sixty ambulances had been converted from private cars by the council's central depot. (PMRS 1985/53/2)

The staff of First Aid Post & Depot No. 3 at Cottage Grove School, Southsea, in 1939 or 1940. They include nurses and rescue squad personnel. Most would have been unpaid volunteers. By 1944, Portsmouth had some 5,400 ARP personnel, but their numbers were decreased as the threat of air raids lessened. (PMRS 2002/615)

An ARP rescue and demolition squad with a requisitioned lorry. These squads were formed to rescue people from partially collapsed, bomb-damaged buildings. The inhabitants might still be alive, but trapped wherever they had been sheltering (under the stairs, for example). Vans and lorries from many local firms were taken over for ARP purposes. (PMRS 1995/73/3)

Rescue workers and a policeman recover a casualty from the remains of a bombed Portsmouth building. This photograph gives some idea of how difficult this job could be, with the ever-present threat that the rubble would collapse further. The bodies of people killed by bombing were often collected by refuse vehicles from the council's central depot. (PMRS 1321A/1/13/17)

Local residents are shown how a stirrup pump works. Neighbourhood groups were set up in Portsmouth during the summer of 1940 to help after air raids. By the end of 1940 there were 861 trained fire parties, each consisting of four to five people. They were equipped with stirrup pumps for use against incendiary bombs, which burnt with an intense flame and could cause severe damage if not extinguished rapidly. (*News 1029*)

| Date | Name | Arrival | Departure | Remarks |
|------|------|---------|-----------|---------|
| June 25 | J.H. Dilbury | 9.30 p.m. | 6 a.m. | 8.40 — 10-30pm |
| | Mr. E. Thompson | 10.30p. | 6 a.m. | 10.45 — 11-25.. |
| | N.K. Blockley | 10.30pm. | 6 a.m. | 11.35pm – 12.4 am |
| | | | | 12.30. — 1.50 am |
| | | | | 3.35 — 4 a.m |
| | | . | | 4.7 — 4.32 an |
| | | | | 4.52 – 5.32 . .. |
| | | | | Remarks:- ''' x ''/ .. ! |
| | Week Commencing 26th June '44. | | | |
| Date | Name | Arrival | Departure | Remarks |
| June 26th | A.J. Jones. | 9-30 P.m. | 6-0 A.m. | Alert 1.45 – 2.30 am. |
| | G. Curtis | 9.45 pm | 6.45 a.m. | |

A page from the Fire Guard log book for Court Lane School, Cosham, for 25 June 1944. Each air-raid alert might be caused by just a single German aircraft passing overhead, but did not necessarily mean an actual attack. The Fire Guard was created in August 1941. Fire Guards did duty on a rota basis, protecting their street or place of work against incendiary bombs. (PMRS 1991/110)

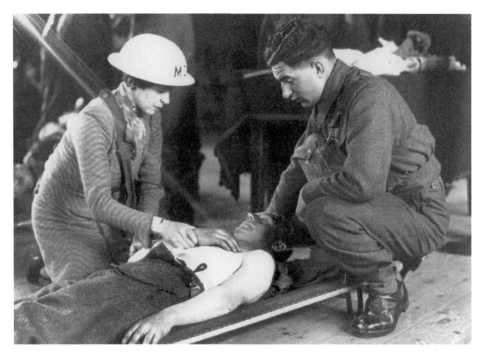

*Above:* Dr Una Mulvany, leader of the first aid party at St George's Square, Portsea, checks on an air-raid casualty. She was awarded the MBE for her services in this role. She wears a white-painted steel helmet to indicate her position, with the letters 'MO' (Medical Officer) indicating that she is a doctor. (*News 1619*)

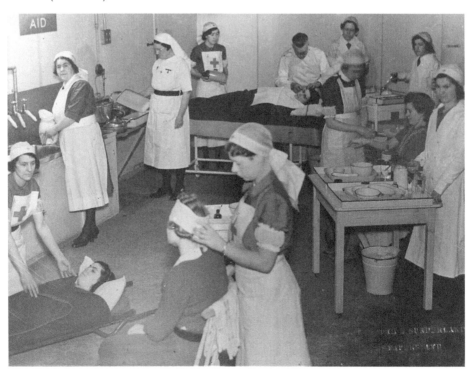

*Opposite below:* First Aid Post No. 1 at St Mary's Hospital, run by Miss Violet Welldon. When the post was bombed and the lights went out, the nurses heard her shout from the next room 'Put your torches on and return to your posts.' Only later did they discover that Miss Welldon had been severely wounded by the explosion, and the doctor with her had been killed. (*News*)

*Right:* Nurse Nora Metcalf in 1943 at the Royal Hospital, Landport. Portsmouth's nurses treated wounded servicemen from the 1940 Dunkirk evacuation, the 1942 Dieppe Raid and the 1944 D-Day Landings, as well as civilians injured in the Blitz. The hospital was badly bombed on 10 January 1941. Whatever happened, a nurse's uniform still had to be neat and tidy at all times! (PMRS EF1990)

*Below:* Canadian fire fighters put on a party at the Royal Hospital at Christmas 1943. All children who had attended the hospital during the year were invited. The first Canadian firemen arrived in Portsmouth in Autumn 1942. They were volunteers from all over Canada, and served in the UK for two years. (PMRS EF1990)

Reserve policemen at Southsea Police Station in 1940 (left to right: -?-, Peter Crisp, Bill Woolven, -?-). They are equipped with steel helmets, which were vital to protect their heads during air raids, particularly from fragments from exploded anti-aircraft shells fired by nearby guns. These would rain down all over the city and could be lethal. (PMRS 1994/597, copyright Goronwy Wynne Evans GM)

Mr A.J. Hickey of New Road, Copnor, wearing his Special Constable's uniform. He worked for Portsmouth and Gosport Gas Company. Specials assisted the regular police in their normal duties, and were also called out in emergencies. They had been involved in ARP preparations since before the war. (PMRS 1983/12/35)

Nine Women Police Auxiliaries standing in a row on the steps at Byculla House (later Brankesmere) at Queens Crescent, Southsea, which·became the Police HQ. They are, left to right, Grace Griffiths, Francis Esther Clarke, Muriel Regina Hart, Stella Blackman, -?-, Mrs Heather, Vivienne Williams, -?-, Gladys Bootes, Senior Auxiliary Doris Mabel Stead. (PMRS 1993/20/6)

Members of the Women's Police Auxiliary march along Pembroke Road, through bomb-damaged
Old Portsmouth. They are followed by a group of firemen. A much higher proportion of Portsmouth's
policemen enlisted in the armed forces than the national average (34 per cent compared to 21.5 per cent).
The remainder were joined in their duties by Women Auxiliaries, Specials and the Police War Reserve.
The tower of Portsmouth Anglican Cathedral can be seen in the background. (PMRS 1993/20/9)

*Right:* Firemen practising with a ladder at the Central Fire Station, Park Road, in 1940. They are (left to right): Horace Graham, Cliffe Park, Eddie Wallace, David Jones, Eric Snook. These regular firemen were part of the city's police force. In wartime they were assisted by members of the Auxiliary Fire Service (AFS). In autumn 1941, all fire services were combined into the National Fire Service. Its creation was the result of problems experienced during the Blitz. (PMRS 2004/2948)

*Below:* AFS (left) and regular firemen draw water from a temporary tank during an exercise in Edinburgh Road in 1940. The group of four regulars in the right foreground (facing the camera, left to right) are Bob Firbank, Tom Lewis, Eddie Wallace, Phil Moseley. (*News*)

*Left:* Fire service messenger Vernon Sellwood from Drayton, aged fifteen, was awarded the British Empire Medal. During the night of 10-11 March 1941, Portsmouth suffered one of its most severe air raids. Vernon helped fight the fires for four hours, and several firemen were killed near him as the bombs continued to fall. Messengers proved vital during the raid of 10-11 January 1941 in particular, as the telephone system was knocked out. (PMRS 2004/580)

*Below:* Auxiliary Fire Service women in 1939. They performed important administrative roles, and three (in shiny coats) were despatch riders. Back row, left to right: -?-, -?-, -?-, Phyl McGregor, -?-, G. Welch. Middle row: -?-, -?-, Joyce Whitfield, -?-, -?-, -?-. Front row: -?-, -?-, Rosina Smith, -?-, H. Hatton, Alice Pitt, -?-, Hilda Perry, Joyce Perry, Celia Broadbridge, -?-. (PMRS 1990/1322/7)

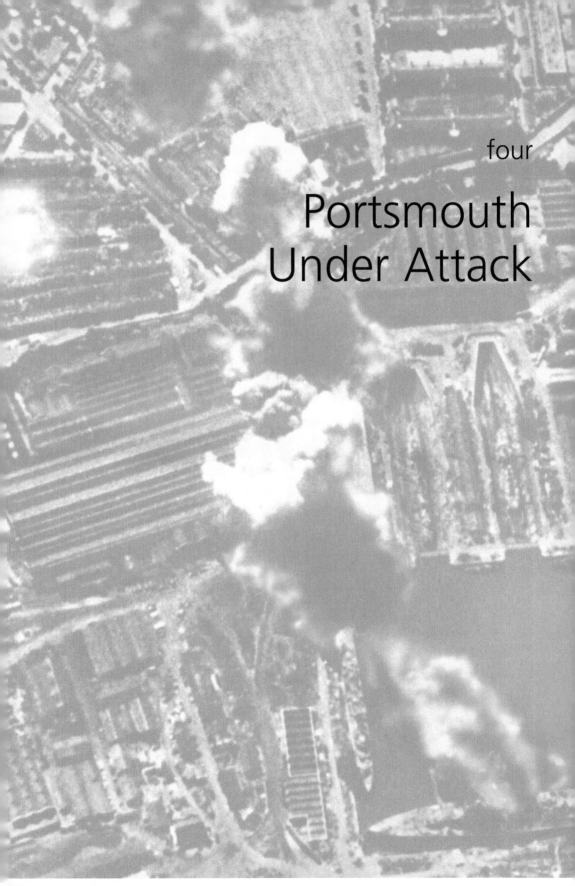

four

# Portsmouth
# Under Attack

The sixty-seven air raids suffered by Portsmouth from July 1940 to July 1944 left the most visible evidence of the city's wartime experiences: 930 people dead, 1,216 hospitalised, and 1,621 with less severe injuries. Just under 10 per cent of the city's 63,000 houses were destroyed, a similar number were seriously damaged, and nearly 69,000 cases of lesser damage were recorded. Each of the 1,581 air-raid warnings – not all of which turned into actual attacks on the city – meant people going into the air-raid shelters and the fear of sudden death and destruction. Due to Portsmouth's importance as a naval base, air attacks on the city were generally not referred to directly in the newspapers or on the radio, but were described as raids on 'a south coast town'. This caused some resentment at the time amongst local people who felt that the city's suffering was not being recognised.

The Luftwaffe (German air force) dropped bombs all over the city. Were the Germans deliberately aiming to kill civilians, or simply inaccurate? At first the Luftwaffe tried to target sites such as docks and factories. However they soon came to think that heavy civilian casualties might cause the British public to call for peace. In addition, in the first half of the war neither side was capable of extremely accurate aerial bombing, especially at night. Non-visual methods of navigation such as dead reckoning or using radio beams (used for example at night or when there was heavy cloud) were inaccurate. On some occasions, German aircraft may also have dropped their bombs early and without trying to hit the target precisely, in order to escape the city's heavy defences (searchlights, anti-aircraft guns, barrage balloons and fighter aircraft).

The usual pattern of behaviour during the Blitz (the bombing raids of 1940-1941) was of everyone pulling together and supporting each other. As common as this was, it would also be inaccurate to suggest that this always happened. Looting from bombed houses was not unknown. 'Trekkers' left the city at the end of every day to seek safety away from the bombing, returning the next morning. While this was understandable, they were criticised by some for leaving their homes unguarded against incendiary bombs.

The figures for the number of bombs dropped on Portsmouth are usually given as 1,320 high explosive (HE) and 38,000 incendiary bombs. In fact, German records state that 40,000 incendiaries were dropped in a single raid alone, on 10-11 January 1941, and that during the whole war 2-3,000 HE bombs were dropped. Sometimes German aircraft mistakenly bombed another location that they thought was Portsmouth. Other bombs fell into the sea, rather than on land, and some of those that did fall on land may not have been recorded precisely. Some of the figures for bombs dropped are given below in tons. The most numerous HE type used by the Luftwaffe was a 250kg bomb (i.e. four bombs per ton), but a variety of types were used on larger raids.

*Opposite above:* After a series of false alarms, the first bombs were dropped on Portsmouth on 11 July 1940 by twenty-four German aircraft seeking to hit the dockyard. They damaged the Blue Anchor pub and nearby buildings in Kingston Crescent. The raid killed nineteen people – including eleven staff at the Drayton Road School first aid post – and left many more wounded. (*News* 943)

*Opposite below:* Residents of Bonfire Corner, Portsea, salvage possessions from their bomb-damaged houses. This area was hit in the second raid on the city, on 12 August 1940. Across the city, thirteen people were killed and 100 wounded in the attack. (*News* 1024)

A German photograph taken during the raid on Portsmouth of 12 August 1940. The battleship HMS *Queen Elizabeth*, then still under construction, can be seen at the bottom (she had a near miss but was not hit). The photograph is taken from a German propaganda booklet aimed at their Italian allies, entitled 'The Admiralty Regrets to Announce', describing how many British ships the Germans were supposedly sinking. It was found in 1942 by Norman Barber from Portsmouth, at a former Italian camp at Tobruk, Libya. He was serving with 155th Light Anti-Aircraft Battery. (PMRS 2006/521)

The view from a German aircraft flying at high altitude during or shortly after a bombing raid on Portsmouth, probably in July or August 1940. Bombs have fallen across Southsea, Landport and Fratton. This photograph illustrates how scattered German bombing often was, even in the daytime. Southsea Common is at the bottom of the photograph. (PMRS 681A/3/1A)

| Warning. | Date. | Time | In Shelter |
|---|---|---|---|
| 70ᵗ | Aug. 21ˢᵗ | 2·40 p.m. – 3·30 p.m. | ---- 50 minutes |
| 71ˢᵗ | Aug. 22ⁿᵈ | 11·28 p.m. – 11·35 p.m. | --- 7 minutes |
| 72ⁿᵈ | Aug. 23ʳᵈ | 3·0 p.m. – 3·25 p.m. | ---- 25 minutes |
| 73ʳᵈ | Aug. 23ʳᵈ | 3·45 p.m. – 4·15 p.m. | ---- ¼ hour. |
| 74ᵗ | Aug. 23ʳᵈ | 6·40 p.m. – 7·34 p.m. | ..... 54 minutes |
| 75ᵗ | Aug. 23ʳᵈ (2 mins later) | 7·36 p.m. – 7·50 p.m. | .... 14 minutes |
| 76ᵗ | Aug. 24ᵗ | 4·20 – 6·0 p.m. (Big raid over Southsea) (we got in for it) | -- 1 hr. 40 min |
| 77ᵗ | Aug. 24ᵗ | 6·10 p.m. – 6·45 p.m. | ---- 35 minute |
| 78ᵗ | Aug. 24ᵗ | 9·15 p.m. – 10·5 p.m. | ----- 50 minutes |
| 79ᵗ | Aug. 24ᵗ | 11·45 p.m. – 4·5 a.m. | ---- 4 hrs. 20 mins |
| 80ᵗ | Aug. 25ᵗ | 9·55 a.m. – 10·30 a.m. | ----- 35 minutes |
| 81ˢᵗ | Aug. 25ᵗ | 9·20 p.m. – 2·17 a.m. | ---- 4 hrs. 57 minute |
| 82ⁿᵈ | Aug. 26ᵗ | 12·50 p.m. – 1·20 p.m. | ------ ½ hour. |
| 83ʳᵈ | Aug. 26ᵗ | 1·50 p.m. – 1·55 p.m. | .... 5 minutes |
| 84ᵗ | Aug. 26ᵗ | 4·10 p.m. – 5·45 p.m. | Raid (Ordnance etc.) got Cumberland ---- 1 hour 35 min |
| 85ᵗ | Aug. 26ᵗ | 10·50 p.m. – 11·17 p.m. | --- 27 mins. |

The air-raid diary of Mrs F. Clarke of Whitwell Road, Southsea. On 24 August 1940 there was a large air raid in which five people in the house opposite her were killed. Across the city, 125 people died and over 100 were seriously injured – the heaviest casualties from a single raid on the UK up to this date. (PMRS 1122A)

Bomb damage to St Alban's church, Copnor Road, on 17 September 1940. The police have set up a diversion until the site has been checked for casualties and unexploded bombs. A single heavy bomb here injured twenty-seven people, four of them seriously, and damaged 424 properties. (*News* 1105)

On 5 December 1940 a bomb hit the Carlton Cinema in Cosham, killing three of the audience and wounding forty more. This was the first of the heavy night raids on Portsmouth. The German aircraft navigated by dead reckoning or by radio direction due to clouds, which decreased the accuracy of their bombing. Across the city, forty-four people were killed and 140 injured. (*News* 1287)

*Below:* The Conway Street area of Landport, seen after a German aircraft dropped a huge 2,500kg 'Max' bomb and a 1,000kg 'Hermann' bomb. The date was 23 December 1940. It has also been suggested that the damage was caused by an aircraft crashing with its bomb load still on board, but no aircraft wreckage was found at the scene. (PMRS 1995/323)

Soldiers check through the rubble of Conway Street School after the 23 December bomb. The civilian casualties were eighteen killed and 169 injured, plus forty wounded in the dockyard. Nineteen streets of houses were destroyed, windows were blown out up to two miles away and hundreds of people were left homeless. (PMRS 1995/320)

The Queen's Hotel and Osborne Road at 11 p.m. on 10 January 1941, during Portsmouth's worst raid of the war. The artist was Graham Cliverd, chief camouflage officer of the Admiralty, who was staying at a nearby hotel. During a lull in the bombing, he made a sketch on which this drawing was based. (PMRS 1997/639)

*Above:* Damage in Palmerston Road, Southsea, after the attack of 10-11 January 1941. The spire of St Jude's church is in the background. Palmerston Road was one of the first areas to be hit. This raid was one of a series of German attacks in that month on ports, although in practice it was usually the civilian population who bore the brunt of the bombing, rather than the docks facilities. (*News*)

The attack was the main air raid on the UK that the Luftwaffe (German air force) made that night. Portsmouth was selected as a target because most of the rest of the country was covered with cloud. Portsmouth's position on the coast was also likely to make the city easier for the bombers to locate in poor conditions. The German bombers were guided by two VHF radio beams which intersected over Southsea Common, a method with an accuracy of about one mile at that range. These radio beams were detected in advance, so the British had some warning that Portsmouth would be attacked.

Although the number of attackers is sometimes given as 300 aircraft, German records show that 153 aircraft claimed to have bombed Portsmouth, dropping 140 tons of high explosive bombs and over 40,000 incendiaries. In total, incendiary bombs caused 2,314 fires, which was simply too many for the fire services to bring under control immediately. By 9 p.m., the fires in Portsmouth could be seen by German aircraft as they crossed the French coast.

*Opposite above:* A view along King's Road, Southsea, in the aftermath of the night raid of 10-11 January 1941. The streets have since been cleared of rubble. The raid took place over a period of seven hours, leaving 171 people dead and 430 injured. (PMRS 1995/331)

A view of the Connaught Drill Hall in Stanhope Road, painted after the raid of 10-11 January by Edward King. The FA Cup (won by Portsmouth in 1939) was stored in the vaults of Lloyds Bank in nearby Commercial Road, and had to be dug out of the rubble after the attack. (PMRS 1945/446)

A mass funeral was held at Kingston Cemetery on 17 January 1941 for some of those killed during the air raid of 10-11 January. The ceremony was attended by Portsmouth's Lord Mayor and Lady Mayoress, Denis and Margaret Daley, as well as many other local dignitaries. (PMRS 1999/744)

*Left:* Soldiers clearing the interior of Portsmouth Guildhall in January 1944, three years after it was burnt to the ground on the night of 10-11 January 1941. It was destroyed by incendiary (fire) bombs, rather than by a high explosive bomb as is sometimes stated. Council workers and firemen extinguished many of the incendiaries that had landed on the roof, but one dropped down a ventilation shaft and proved impossible to put out. The city council subsequently took over the Royal Beach Hotel on the Southsea seafront for its offices. (PMRS 608A/24)

*Opposite above:* Prime Minister Winston Churchill – seen here with the Lord Mayor – visited Portsmouth on 31 January 1941 to see the bomb damage for himself. Churchill was given the Freedom of the City that August. (*News*)

King George VI and Queen Elizabeth inspect the Civil Defence services outside the Royal Beach Hotel on 6 February 1941. The King and Queen also inspected the interior of the burnt-out Guildhall, and toured around the city to visit emergency centres, Police and ARP personnel. (*News*)

Firemen tackle fires in Queen Street, Landport, in the aftermath of a raid (probably in early 1941). The problems posed to emergency services by rubble on the roads are evident. Bombing often broke water mains, so that there was not enough water to put out fires. Around sixty water mains were cut during the raid of 10-11 January 1941, and at the same time a low tide prevented firemen from getting additional water from the sea. (PMRS 1321A/1/13/6)

March 1941 saw a Luftwaffe policy of repeated air attacks on individual cities, including Portsmouth. There were five night raids on the city in one week. The attack of 10-11 March was the heaviest raid on the UK (in terms of tonnage of high explosive bombs dropped) since the previous December. It was the thirty-seventh raid on Portsmouth, and the city's 481st alert of the war. The crews of 238 German bomber aircraft claimed to have hit Portsmouth, dropping 193 tons of high explosive bombs and over 46,000 incendiaries in a seven-hour attack. Fires were started in the Dockyard, at the Royal Naval Barracks, at Vosper's shipbuilding works and elsewhere. The casualties were ninety-three people killed, 164 seriously wounded and eighty-three more lightly injured.

*Right:* April 1941 was also a month of heavy raids. This 'Victory Cross' was erected on the site of the parish hall of St Cuthbert's church, Copnor. The church was already badly damaged when a land mine fell in Hayling Avenue on 17 April 1941. A land mine was a sea mine converted so that it could be dropped from an aircraft as a huge bomb, with a parachute attached to slow its descent. That night's attack was made by 249 aircraft which dropped 346 tons of high explosive bombs and 46,000 incendiaries. (PMRS 1318A/2/29)

*Below:* An aerial photograph taken by the RAF in October 1945, showing the area of Lake Road, Portsea. Empty spaces can be seen where bomb-damaged houses have been cleared away. Bombsites were common throughout Portsmouth for years after the war. (PMRS SA/CC/DG)

Two women use a pram to salvage possessions from their bombed house. Air raids left many people homeless. Despite stories of communities pulling together and the 'Blitz spirit', looting was not unknown, and some people returned to their bomb-damaged houses to find that valuable possessions had been stolen. (*News* 2660)

An open-air canteen infront of the war memorial in Guildhall Square. These canteens were often run by the Women's Voluntary Service (WVS). The Council had kitchens in Heidelberg Road, Southsea, that could supply hot meals for 2,000 people after a raid. (*News* 1336)

The Lady Mayoress, Lady Margaret Daley, with four young air-raid victims in September 1943. Their new clothes were bought with money that had originally been sent to Queen Elizabeth by four young Scottish girls. Lady Daley organised clothing depots that distributed more than 180,000 garments to 34,321 people during the war. (*News*)

Council workmen cover bomb-blasted windows at Shakespeare Road, Fratton. Rest centres were set up across Portsmouth to care for people who had been left homeless by air raids. During the war, 16,000 people who had lost their homes used the centres, which were run by volunteers. (PMRS 1981/355)

Local people emerge from a communal air-raid shelter at Commercial Road, Mile End. Some communal shelters were built above ground using brick. Those constructed quickly at the start of the war were sometimes of poor quality. This one is apparently below ground, a much safer method of construction that was not available in low-lying parts of Portsmouth. (*News*)

*Left:* An Anderson Shelter amongst the rubble of bombed houses in around 1941. Although these shelters were of basic construction – simply heavy-duty corrugated steel panels which were half-buried in the ground, with earth piled on top – they often survived considerable bomb damage. However they could not protect against a direct hit. (PMRS 1994/595, copyright Goronwy Wynne Evans GM)

*Opposite above:* In 1941, two separate tunnel systems were dug as air-raid shelters under Portsdown Hill, at London Road and Wymering. They were around 100ft (30m) below the surface of the hill. This map of the London Road tunnels is from the shelter ticket issued to eight-year old Sheila Knight of Beresford Road, North End. (PMRS 2001/707)

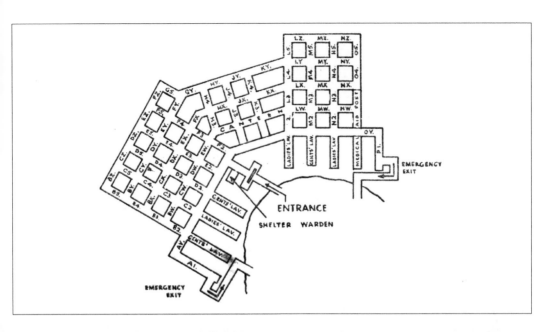

A scene inside the Portsdown tunnel shelters on 17 December 1942, during a Christmas party for 700 local children. The two shelters could hold over 5,000 people. Priority was given to those who did not have their own shelters, families with children, older people and those with an illness. (*News* 2393)

*Above:* A defused German 'Satan' 1800kg bomb is recovered at Torrington Road, North End, in 1941. Bombs that did not explode on impact often buried themselves deep into the ground and had to be dealt with by bomb disposal teams. There were also delayed action bombs, designed to go off several hours after they had hit the ground. (PMRS DF/P.17/11/9)

A clean-up operation in progress in the area of Dunbar Road, Milton, on 26 March 1943. The photograph illustrates the terrible destructive effect that a single large bomb could have; it has left a massive crater and blown the roofs and walls off nearby houses. Removing the rubble from damaged properties was a huge task that had to be done before any rebuilding could take place. (PMRS DF/ P.17/11/4)

*Opposite below:* A view east along Yorke Street, Southsea, as demolition work is carried out on 11 January 1944. This area was hit by high explosive bombs in August 1940, and January and March 1941. (PMRS 608A/28)

A view to the west from Commercial Road in 1943 or 1944, looking across the wasteland that was previously Spring and Charlotte Streets. The rubble from bombed buildings has mostly been cleared away, leaving only a group of brick-built air-raid shelters. (PMRS 608A/10)

A sketch by Mrs V. Pearse showing King's Road, Southsea, in July 1943. On the right is the tower of Elm Grove Baptist church, which was burnt out in the raid of 10-11 January 1941. The bombsite in the foreground has wooden railings around it to prevent anyone falling into the hole during the blackout. (PMRS 1945/217/2)

*Right:* Soldiers working on the hardcore dump at St Paul's Square, Southsea. The rubble was collected from the ruins of bombed local houses, and was then used in the foundations of various construction projects. (PMRS 2005/1202)

*Below:* Lorries carry hardcore across to Gosport on the Floating Bridge on 5 December 1943. The rubble was used to build embarkation ramps ('hards') in Gosport and Stokes Bay for loading vehicles for D-Day. It seems somehow appropriate that many of the Allied troops departing to liberate Europe did so over the rubble of bomb-damaged Portsmouth. (PMRS 2005/1197)

The scene in Locksway Road, Milton, after the first of two V-1 flying bombs hit Portsmouth, on 25 June 1944, causing serious injuries to fourteen people. The V-1's engine cut out after a pre-set time, at which point it fell to earth. The first V-1s were launched at England on 13 June 1944, in an attempt to undermine civilian morale and force the Allies to make peace. (*News* 2917)

The second V-1 hit Stamshaw on 15 July 1944, leaving fifteen people dead and eighty-two injured. This is a rooftop view from a house in Winstanley Road, looking towards Newcomen Road and Whale Island. The huge hole where the V-1 fell can be seen in the distance. (PMRS 1964/297)

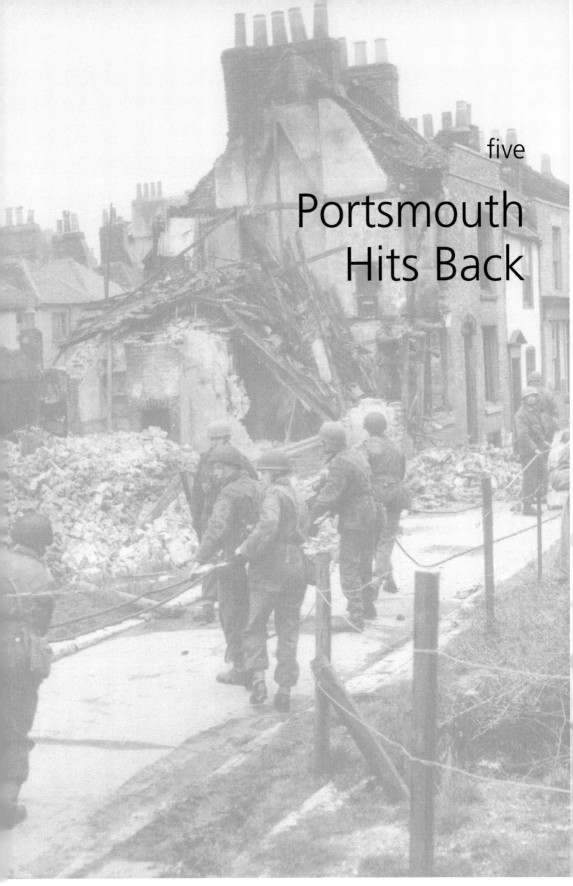

five

# Portsmouth Hits Back

Portsmouth's famous connections with the Royal Navy sometimes overshadow its equally important links with the Army, which for centuries provided the garrison that protected the area's naval facilities. These associations with the armed forces continued during the Second World War. Not only did many Portsmouth people join the armed services, but the city also played its part in fighting the war.

After the French defeat in May–June 1940, Allied troops were rescued from France at Dunkirk and other ports. Even the Hayling Island ferries and other small craft went to take part in these evacuations, bringing some of the troops back to Portsmouth. Wounded soldiers from the August 1942 Dieppe Raid were also brought back to Portsmouth. The 'Cockleshell Heroes' of the Royal Marine Boom Patrol Detachment were based at Lumps Fort in Southsea and trained in the area prior to their attacks on shipping at Bordeaux in December 1942. Men of the Combined Operations Pilotage Parties (COPPS) trained on Hayling Island for their task of reconnoitring enemy-held beaches prior to invasion. Many naval bases were set up in the area in wartime, such as HMS *Northney* which used several holiday camps on Hayling Island. With the onset of regular bombing raids, parts of the Dockyard and of some naval facilities were moved to safer places outside the city. Some departments from HMS *Vernon* were moved from Gunwharf Quays (as it is now known) to Brighton, and the Navy's Navigation School moved to Southwick.

The city's vulnerability to German bombing raids meant that few warships were built at the dockyard during the war, but it did play a vital role in refitting and repairing ships. The period around D-Day (the Allied landings in Normandy on 6 June 1944) was perhaps Portsmouth's finest hour. In June and July 1944, 418 ships and landing craft were repaired in Portsmouth Dockyard, most of which had taken part in the Normandy Landings. The Allied fleet for Normandy was supplied with food, drink and armaments from bases on the Gosport side of the Harbour: the Royal Clarence Victualling Yard, and the Royal Naval Armament Depots at Priddy's Hard, Frater and Bedenham. HMS *Hornet* at Haslar Lake, and the nearby former submarine station of HMS *Dolphin*, were assembly points for motor torpedo boats and similar small craft.

Portsmouth men and women also served overseas in many other campaigns and parts of the world throughout the war, from North Africa to the Far East, from the Atlantic to the Pacific. Locally-raised units included the 57th Heavy Anti-Aircraft Regiment of the Royal Artillery (a Territorial Army unit that defended the area during the Blitz, and later served in North Africa and Italy), or the battalions of the Hampshire Regiment as well as the many Portsmouth-based warships. However most local people served in hundreds of other units that did not necessarily have a specific local connection.

*Above:* HMS *Nelson* entering Portsmouth Harbour in around 1937. She was built under the 1922 Washington Naval Treaty, resulting in her unusual design of three forward turrets. Her war service included the Mediterranean, Atlantic Convoys and the Normandy Landings. After 1940, air attacks on Portsmouth meant that few ships of this size used the port. (PMRS 1976/158, courtesy of Royal Naval Museum)

*Right:* Airborne soldiers help clear bomb-damaged houses in Silver Street, Southsea. Sailors, Royal Marines and soldiers were often brought in to help deal with the aftermath of air raids. (PMRS 1997/429)

A ceremony was held in Guildhall Square in June 1942 to mark United Nations Day. It was attended by locally-based servicemen and women, as well as residents. The parade included Royal Marine bandsmen, Wrens, sailors of the Royal Navy and Royal Indian Navy – illustrating the variety of armed forces

personnel present in the Portsmouth area – as well as the Civil Defence, Police and Fire Services. At this time, the term 'United Nations' was used to mean all the Allied countries that were fighting against the Axis powers (Germany, Italy and Japan). (*News*)

The Southern Railway paddle steamer *Whippingham* (seen here in around 1950) was used for excursions and as a Portsmouth-Ryde ferry. Her wartime naval service included rescuing troops during the 1940 evacuations from Dunkirk, operating as a minesweeper, and then acting as an anti-aircraft vessel during the D-Day Landings. (PMRS 2006/611)

Wrens – as members of the Women's Royal Naval Service or WRNS were known – on parade in 1939 at HMS *Vernon* (now Gunwharf Quays). At its greatest size, there were nearly 75,000 women in the WRNS. Many of them did jobs that before the war had been considered unsuitable for women. (PMRS 2002/591)

Boat's crew Wrens operating a steam picket boat from HMS *Vernon* in Portsmouth Harbour, May 1944. They are (left to right) Diana Smelt (later Cottam), Joan Beale, and Dorothy Greenleaf. Boom Tower House and Tower House – marked here with an 'X' – were their lodgings. Wrens also did jobs such as driving, meteorology, communications, or working with armaments. (PMRS 2003/1646)

Sailors parade in front of HMS *Victory* during a visit to Portsmouth Dockyard by King George VI on 16 November 1944. *Victory* sustained some damage from a bomb that fell into her dry dock. On one occasion, German radio claimed that the ship had been destroyed by a bomb, and the Admiralty had to issue a denial. (PMRS 1994/31/4)

Band leader Harry Sutton (in shirt sleeves, seated behind drums) and his band entertain servicemen and servicewomen at Hayling Island Services Hostel between 1939-1940. Members of all three services attended the band's regular dances. (PMRS 2001/309)

The YMCA hut, situated opposite the Guildhall, was opened in March 1940 and provided refreshments and an enquiry office. It was run by Mr Carrick, the bearded man under the 'C' of the left-hand lower lettering 'YMCA'. He is seen here with other staff and some of the servicemen who used the building. (PMRS 2002/588)

Sailors of the Royal Indian Navy training at Stamshaw in 1942. India was still under British rule, and the Indian Navy operated in the Atlantic and Mediterranean as well as closer to home. In the original photograph, the distinctive chalk cliffs of Portsdown Hill in the background were obliterated by the wartime censor, to disguise the location. (IWM A 10554)

Free French leader General Charles de Gaulle inspects French sailors at their camp, probably near Emsworth. Following the French surrender in June 1940, several thousand British servicemen took control of thirty-four French ships that had fled to Portsmouth, including the battleship *Courbet*. Their intention was to prevent the ships from returning to France and being seized by the Germans. (*News* 2322)

US Navy photographer Lieutenant Fred Gerretson (left), Photographer's Mate 1st Class Bob Greenawalt (with camera) and two other US sailors with Portsmouth children in Spring 1944. For children, meeting foreign servicemen was an exciting aspect of the war, especially if they gave out presents such as chocolate. Gerretson and Greenawalt were official photographers on Utah Beach on D-Day. (PMRS 1997/365, copyright US Navy)

African-American troops at Cosham or Hilsea prepare coffee rations for other GIs (as American soldiers were known). The Americans drank coffee, not tea like the British. The US Army kept black and white troops separate at all times, a policy that led to strong objections from some British people. (*News* 2898)

Sherman tanks and other vehicles of a British unit parked along a road just north of Portsmouth at Horndean, shortly before D-Day. All would have been quickly camouflaged against enemy aircraft. In fact, the Allied defences were so strong that virtually no German planes were able to cross the south coast and spot the preparations for D-Day. (*News* 2888)

Men of C Company, 1st Battalion, the Lancashire Regiment in camp before D-Day at either Padnell (north of Waterlooville) or at Queen's Inclosure, Cowplain. The corporal, second from the left in the front row, is wearing the triangular badge of the 3rd Division to which this unit belonged. These troops landed at Sword Beach on D-Day. (PMRS 2001/1475/1)

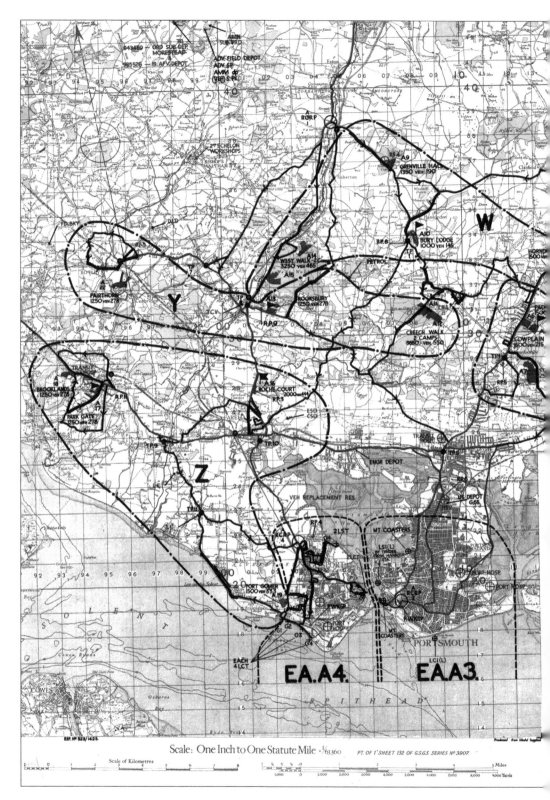

Scale: One Inch to One Statute Mile · 1/63,360   PT. OF 1" SHEET 132 OF G.S.G.S. SERIES Nº 3907

Scale of Kilometres

NOT TO BE REPRODUCED

Copy No 251

SECRET

## AREA 'A'

### OVERLORD

### ADMINISTRATIVE MAP

### 1. MAY 1944.

SHEET ONE OF FIVE

## LEGEND

| | |
|---|---|
| | MARSHALLING AREA H.Q. |
| | SUB-AREA H.Q. |
| | CAMPS (Nº Shown – eg. A.I.) |
| ○RCRP | ROAD CONVOY REGULATING POINT |
| • TP | TRAFFIC POST |
| | VEHICLE PARK or STANDINGS |
| | ONE-WAY ROUTE |
| | ONE-WAY OPERATIONAL – TWO-WAY ADM. & CIVILIAN |
| | TWO-WAY ROUTE |
| | SUB-AREA BOUNDARY |
| | EMBARKATION AREA BOUNDARY |
| PETROL | PETROL OIL & LUBRICANT DUMP |
| RP | RECOVERY POST (VEHICLE) |
| P. WKSP | PORT WORKSHOP |
| • | DETRAINING STATION |
| PW | PRISONERS of WAR CAGE |
| + | HARDS (Nº Shown – e.g. S.I.) }Capacities |
| ⊕ | EMBARKATION POINTS } given |
| ENGR DEPOT | ENGINEER DEPOT |

## EQUIVALENT INSTALLATIONS

| BRITISH | U. S. |
|---|---|
| ORDNANCE DEPOT | ADVANCE FIELD DEPOT & ADVANCE SHOP |
| SUB VEHICLE RESERVE DEPOT | VEHICLE SUPPLY PARK |
| AMMUNITION SUPPLY DEPOT | AMMUNITION DISTRIBUTING POINT |
| LIGHT REPAIR SECTION | |
| | ENGINEER DUMP |
| DETAIL ISSUE DEPOT | QUARTER-MASTER DISTRIBUTING POINT |
| FIELD BAKERY | QUARTER-MASTER BAKERY |
| COMMAND SUPPLY DEPOT | |
| EMBARKATION SUPPLY DEPOT | |
| | POST EXCHANGE DUMP |
| RECEPTION STATION | |
| EMS TRANSIT HOSPITAL | FIELD HOSPITAL |
| EMS PORT HOSPITAL | STATION HOSPITAL |
| MILITARY HOSPITAL | GENERAL HOSPITAL |
| | MEDICAL DISTRIBUTING POINT |
| | FIRST AID POST |
| | AMBULANCE POST |
| | SIGNAL SUPPLY DUMP |
| | SIGNAL REPAIR SHOP |
| | CHEMICAL WARFARE DUMP |
| TROOP CARRYING VEHICLES | |
| LOAD CARRIERS | |
| | ENGINEER BRIDGING DEPOT |

ED BY CENTRE
UB COMMITTEE
APRIL 1944

(SIGNED) P.W. KEMP WELCH
LT. COL. AQMG (OPS)

(SIGNED) G.M. BOSTOCK COL FA
PLANNING DIVISION SBS

69/1995/1

A map of the D-Day marshalling area and embarkation zone around Portsmouth and Gosport, known as Area A. The markings show the camps further inland where troops waited in the weeks before D-Day, and the routes down to the two embarkation areas (EA): A3 (Portsmouth and Southsea) and A4 (Gosport and Stokes Bay). For D-Day, nearly 27,000 troops and 4,200 vehicles were loaded onto 290 landing craft in the Portsmouth-Gosport sector. By 9 August 1944, 171,922 troops and 42,926 vehicles had embarked from this area. (PMRS 1995/69/1)

Two lines of Phoenix caissons for the Mulberry Harbours, created by the Allies off Normandy after D-Day. The Phoenixes were hollow concrete constructions, up to 60 feet (18 metres) tall, which were sunk in lines to create breakwaters. Twenty Phoenixes were built at Portsmouth Dockyard, fourteen at Stokes Bay and four on Hayling Island. (PMRS 1990/24/11)

A flag given to the crew of a Grenadier Guards tank, which was parked outside the Bedhampton home of four-year old Shirley Whittle at the time of D-Day. The crew flew it on their vehicle all the way to Germany in May 1945. Soldiers waiting to leave for Normandy were often welcomed into local people's houses for a bath or a meal. (PMRS 2005/708)

Vehicles embark onto an LCT (Landing Craft, Tank) at Gosport in June 1944, not long after D-Day. A concrete 'hard' (embarkation ramp) has been built here to facilitate loading. HMS *Vernon* (now Gunwharf Quays) is in the background on the left, and HMS *Dolphin* in Gosport (now the RN Submarine Museum) is at the rear right. At this time, both were used as bases for motor torpedo boats and similar small craft. (PMRS 2004/3903)

Over 130,000 Allied troops and thousands of vehicles were landed in Normandy from the sea on D-Day, followed by hundreds of thousands more over the subsequent months. In order to maintain this huge flow of troops, 130 embarkation hards were built along the south coast of England so that the larger landing craft could load vehicles directly from the beaches. Hards were built at Gosport, Hardway and Stokes Bay, and these sites were therefore important for loading large numbers of tanks and other vehicles.

The LCT and the larger LST (Landing Ship, Tank) were the two main vessels for moving vehicles over to Normandy. Despite their names, the LCT and LST were not intended solely to carry tanks, but all types of vehicles; up to sixty in the case of an LST. The vehicles seen here are reversing on, so that they will be able to drive out forwards on arrival at Normandy.

British soldiers make their way along South Parade Pier, led by a member of the movement control staff. At the end of the pier they will embark onto a landing craft bound for Normandy. In the background is the Royal Beach Hotel, occupied since 1941 as the headquarters of the City Council. (*News* 2859)

Royal Engineers prepare to embark onto a landing craft on one of several temporary piers erected alongside South Parade Pier. This and the adjacent photographs were taken after D-Day, but there would have been similar scenes here immediately before the invasion. (*News* 2945)

More British soldiers on their way to Normandy after D-Day; probably Beach Group troops of 5th Battalion, The King's (Liverpool) Regiment. They are aboard an American-crewed landing craft and are wearing lifebelts. The soldiers' faces reflect the mixed emotions of the troops: enthusiasm that D-Day had at last arrived, but uncertainty or even fear over what lay ahead. (*News* 2910)

# Tuesday 6 ☺

THE INVASION OF EUROPE STARTED TODAY BETWEEN 6 AND 8 A.M. British & American troops landed in Normandie on the Cherbourg Peninsula. They've got a foothold & everything is going according to plan. I was in the Invasion Sweep at work & my day was today so I won it. I received £2. 12s. 6d. I'm going to put it in Salute The Soldier Week which is from 10th – 17th June. There were lots of news flashes came over the radio at work & General Eisenhower gave a short speech. All the landing craft have gone from Hayling (I should say Langstone Harbour) & everywhere is so quiet now all the vehicles ect. have gone.

*Above:* In her diary entry for 6 June 1944, Dorothy Hinde of Portsmouth remarked on how quiet it was, now that most vehicles and ships had departed for Normandy. She was lucky enough to win the sweepstake amongst her workmates to guess the date of D-Day, and generously planned to put her winnings towards the Salute the Soldier fundraising campaign in support of the Army. She was an apprentice draughtswoman at Airspeed. (PMRS 1514A/1/1)

Bad weather forced the postponement of D-Day by twenty-four hours from the planned date of 5 June 1944. The Allied weather forecasters predicted that the weather on 6 June would improve slightly, so that the landings could take place. General Eisenhower gave the order that the landings should be made on 6 June.

In early 1944, it was no secret that the Allies would soon land in north-west Europe. However almost no-one – apart from the top Allied commanders and the planners – knew when or where D-Day would take place. Fortunately these secrets were kept from the Germans. All along the south coast of England, many local people had observed the troops and ships gathering for D-Day. Yet most of them were taken by surprise by the landings.

*Opposite above:* The naval plotting room of the Combined Operations Underground Headquarters, in tunnels underneath Fort Southwick. This and the adjacent rooms gathered information about naval operations in the English Channel. (*News* 3213A)

*Opposite below:* Admiral Sir Bertram Ramsay (left) and General Dwight D. 'Ike' Eisenhower around the time of D-Day. They are outside Southwick House, just north of Portsmouth, which became Ramsay's headquarters in April 1944. Eisenhower (Supreme Allied Commander), Ramsay (Allied Naval Commander), General Sir Bernard Montgomery (Allied Ground Forces Commander) and other Allied leaders met here in the days before D-Day. Led by Eisenhower, they took the fateful decision to launch the invasion on 6 June 1944. (IWM H 39152)

The Dickin Medal – known as the animals' Victoria Cross – awarded to Gustav the pigeon. Battling against a headwind, Gustav flew back to Thorney Island on the morning of D-Day, bearing a message that the first troops had landed safely. Gustav had been bred by Frederick Jackson from Cosham. Gustav's leg ring is on the medal ribbon, and Mr Jackson's National Pigeon Service badge is also in the photograph. (Courtesy of Mrs Alice Pledger)

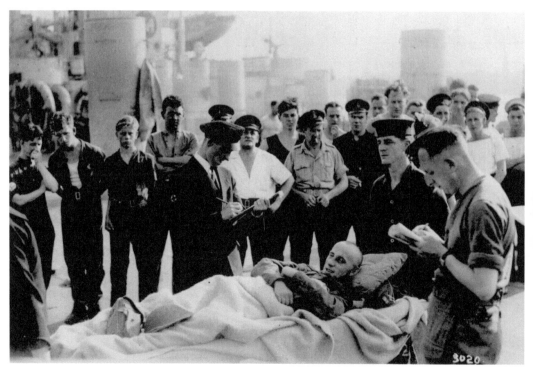

Sailors watch as a wounded soldier from Normandy is carried ashore. The more severely wounded troops were taken immediately to local hospitals. Those able to travel were sent on hospital trains from Fratton Goods Yard to hospitals further inland. By the end of July 1944, nearly 12,000 wounded troops had been landed at Portsmouth Dockyard alone. (*News* 3020)

*Above:* Young German prisoners of war from Normandy, guarded by American troops, arrive in the Portsmouth area, watched by a curious crowd. Prisoners were put in temporary holding camps before being moved inland. (*News* 3267)

*Right:* Victor Stewart, the wartime photographer for Portsmouth's newspaper, *The Evening News*. He took many of the best photographs of wartime Portsmouth. He is wearing a US Army war correspondent's uniform, with which he was issued shortly before D-Day, presumably to make it easier to take photographs of the troops. (*News*)

Landing Craft, Tank (LCT) No. 979 refitting in dry dock at Portsmouth Dockyard after D-Day. The superstructure of the LCT still bears the double-triangle badge of the British 3rd Division, whose troops it carried to Sword Beach on D-Day. The photograph was taken by the LCT's commander, Lieutenant Phillips William Doleman Winkley. (PMRS 1993/14/1)

Beer labels relating to a visit to Normandy in August 1944 by Roderick Kilgour. He was sent to do work in France for the Mine Design Department, based at Leigh Park House. He has marked on the labels (which are from bottles of Brickwood's Brown Brew beer) the place and date where they were drunk. (PMRS 1995/55)

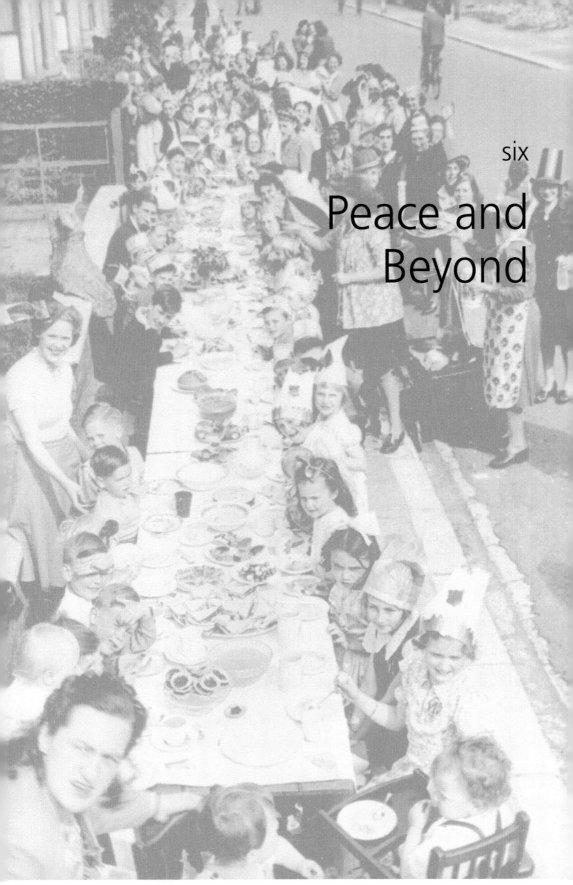

# six

# Peace and Beyond

The announcement of the end of the war against Germany was greeted with great celebration, and 8 May 1945 was designated VE Day (Victory in Europe Day). German forces in Europe had signed a series of surrender documents over the preceding days. VJ Day (Victory over Japan Day) was on 15 August 1945, the day after Japan had accepted the Allied terms of surrender.

VE Day and VJ Day meant different things to different people. For many, the main emotion was of course joy that the fighting was coming to an end. Others thought of friends or relatives who had been killed. On VE Day, some people worried about members of their family who were still serving in the Far East, since the war against Japan showed no sign of ending. Servicemen in Europe were also aware that if the fighting in the Far East continued much longer, many of them would be sent out to that theatre of war to take part in the invasion of Japan. The atomic bombs that were dropped on Hiroshima and Nagasaki brought the war to a close.

For some people the feeling of relief at the end of the fighting was accompanied by uncertainty as to what would happen next: perhaps their home had been destroyed, or they were worried about whether they would get their old job back. The end of the war did not automatically return things to the way that they had been in 1939. British prisoners of war liberated by the advancing Allied armies were rapidly sent home, and often faced a difficult task in readjusting to everyday life. British servicemen and women were slowly demobilised (or 'demobbed', as leaving the armed forces was known). However the hundreds of thousands of soldiers, sailors and airmen could not all be released to civilian life at once. Although the war ended in 1945, some Portsmouth men and women did not return home until 1946 or later.

The war, and the rebuilding that came after it, forever changed the face of Portsmouth. Although the war had caused terrible destruction, the city authorities also saw it as an opportunity to build a better-designed, 'modern' city, with green spaces and sufficient facilities for all residents. On 11 February 1941, a month after the worst air raid on Portsmouth, a committee was established to begin considering the rebuilding of the city. The basis of the plan was that the population density of Portsmouth should be drastically reduced to seventy inhabitants per acre by moving many people off Portsea Island (in 1939 the most congested areas such as Portsea had 200 residents per acre). However the city's limited finances, a shortage of trained architects, and opposition by local traders to major revisions to commercial areas, all acted to limit the speed and scope of the rebuilding. Ten years after the war, the council had built 9,000 new houses to replace those damaged by bombing. Many thousands more that were considered to be sub-standard housing were also subsequently knocked down. Despite the coming of peace, Portsmouth would still face many challenges in the years ahead.

The announcement of the end of the war against Germany was greeted with great celebration on VE Day, 8 May 1945. Children in Cumberland Road, Fratton, marked VE Day with a fancy dress party. (PMRS 1993/507)

Local children celebrate VE Day at the junction of Kassasin Street and Worsley Street, Eastney. They are dancing around a bonfire and are about to burn a dummy of the Nazi leader, Adolf Hitler. Hitler had committed suicide on 30 April. (PMRS EF1161)

A VE Day street party in progress at Worsley Street, Eastney. After so many years of wartime shortages and rationing, producing enough party food required considerable planning and preparation by the families in the street. National flags of the Allied countries have been hung up across the road. In the background is the loopholed wall of the Royal Marines barracks. (PMRS EF1161)

A VE Day fancy dress party in Wilson Road, Stamshaw. Back row, from left to right: Hazel and Olive Martin, Pearl White, -?-. Second row: Jeanie Ayton/Hayton, others unknown. Third row: Doris Bealing, -?-, -?-, -?-,-?-, Norma Carter, others unknown. Fourth row: Margaret Bealing, Teddy Penwarden?, -?-, Joyce, Stella Smith, Rosemary Gale, Brenda Voysey, Joyce Ashman. Front row: -?-, -?-, -?-, Tony Voysey, Harry Carter. (PMRS 1994/53/2)

A good turnout at a VE Day street party in Timpson Street, Landport. The photographer was Laurence Snellgrove. Included in the picture are Joyce Brown (standing at far left), Alice Christopher (the lady kneeling in front of her), Eileen Heather and Sheila Christopher (the two children immediately to the right of Alice). (PMRS 1994/323)

*Left:* Bunting, flags and food are set out to mark VE Day in Aylesbury Road, North End. As well as the many street parties, there was a service of thanksgiving on VE Day morning in Guildhall Square, and a much wilder celebration in the square that evening. (PMRS 1993/482)

*Below:* Not all VE Day celebrations took the form of street parties. Here the residents of Hilltop Crescent, Widley, burn their blackout curtains and the mattresses from their air-raid shelters, which they no longer needed. This was a celebration that people would not have to go down to the hated air-raid shelters again. Life could begin to return to normal. (PMRS 1985/50/2)

*Right:* Street parties were also held for VJ Day, 15 August 1945, which marked the end of the struggle against Japan and the end of the Second World War as a whole. This one is at Milford Road, Landport. (PMRS 2002/608/2)

*Below:* A handmade card sent by Mr 'Scottie' Scott to his wife Frances from Germany, where he was serving in the Royal Signals, to let her know that he would soon be coming home to be demobilised. (PMRS 2003/1642)

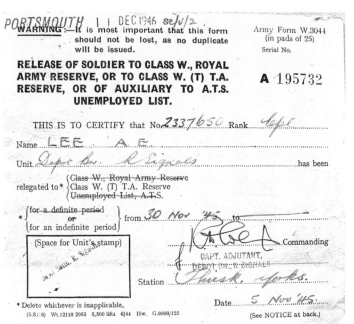

A release certificate authorising the demobilisation of a Portsmouth-born soldier, Corporal A.E. Lee of the Royal Signals, dated 5 November 1945. As a school teacher, he was in one of a number of groups that had priority for leaving the armed forces. (PMRS 1985/107/1)

*Below:* Sailors being demobilised at Portsdown Motor Garage, Northern Road, Cosham. The process apparently took only fifteen minutes, a rapid pace that (the photograph suggests) perhaps left these old salts wondering about the speed of the changes. (*News* 3311)

Demobbed sailors show off their new clothes. Men were provided with a full set of clothing, including a suit and raincoat, while women leaving the armed forces or munitions factories received cash and clothing coupons so that they could choose their own clothes. (*News* 3309)

One of several proposed – but never fulfilled – designs for rebuilding the area around Portsmouth Guildhall and Portsmouth and Southsea train station. The area looks quite different today. A committee to plan the rebuilding of Portsmouth had been established as far back as February 1941. (PMRS)

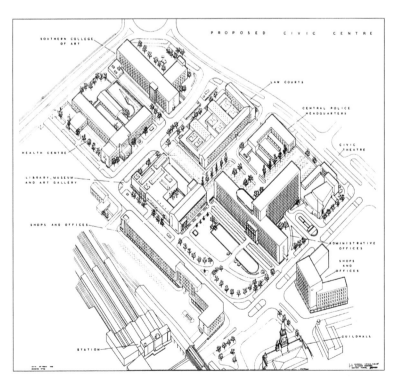

An aerial photograph of bomb-damaged Portsmouth, taken by *Daily Sketch* cameraman Stanley Devon and published in that newspaper on 3 May 1946. It illustrates the extent of the bomb damage and the enormity of the task of reconstruction faced by the city. Many bombsites had been cleared of rubble before the end of the war. The Guildhall can be seen at top left. Work to restore it began in 1955, and it reopened in 1958. (PMRS 1997/496)

**By Chic Young**

DO AS I SAY | DON'T TELL ME A FELLOW HAS TO WASH HIS NECK AND EARS JUST TO CALL ON A | EMILY CAN'T YOU TELL ME WHAT YOU WANT OVER THE PHONE?

*S*OME idea of the price Portsmouth paid for being a great naval port and a front line city is given in this aerial view by "*Daily Sketch*" cameraman Stanley Devon. In 67 raids the city got 1,320

A view over Palmerston Road in 1952, with Stanley Street turning off to the left in the middle distance. Much of this area was destroyed in the night raid of 10-11 January 1941. The Commercial Road area also saw considerable rebuilding work after the war. (PMRS Q66)

Prefabricated buildings (prefabs) on Portsdown Hill. They consisted of an aluminium frame and an asbestos roof, bolted to a concrete base. In November 1945 there were 10,000 people in Portsmouth who needed to be rehoused. The first prefabs were ready by July 1945, and by 1947 over 700 had been put up. The Portsdown Park flats were subsequently built on this site. (PMRS 138A/9/1)

Prefabs in Tamworth Road, Baffins, March 1964, taking advantage of spare space to house those made homeless by the Blitz. The prefabs were generally popular with people who lived in them. (PMRS W14)

British Iron & Steel Federation (BISF) houses under construction in Paulsgrove after the war. Nearly 1,000 of these steel-framed buildings were constructed there, and many are still *in situ*. Other new types that were used to increase the availability of housing were Easiform and Howard houses. (*News*)

An aerial view over Paulsgrove, showing the many houses that were built after the war. The future line of the M27 can be seen extending off to the top left corner of the photograph. Prefabs have been set up where the motorway would be constructed in future, as it was known that their time there was limited. (PMRS AF68)

The end of the war did not bring an immediate end to wartime rationing and shortages. Here local people are given a present of beef, part of a large shipment sent as a gift to the city by A.M. Carpenter of Christchurch, New Zealand, in May 1950. Coal was also in short supply after the war. (*News*)

A wartime SWS (Static Water Supply) sign at the junction of Langstone and Milton Roads, Copnor. SWS were steel or concrete reservoirs filled with water, for use by fire-fighters in case the water mains were broken by bombing during an air raid. This and the following four photographs were taken in 2006. (Author)

One of a large number of Anderson Shelters that were re-used as sheds at the allotments off Locksway Road, Milton. Anderson Shelters and brick-built shelters are also still in place in the gardens of a number of Portsmouth houses. (Author)

Concrete anti-tank blocks still line the roadside at Ferry Road in Eastney, on the way to the Hayling Island ferry. Langstone Harbour could have provided a sheltered point for German vessels to unload troops during an invasion, and these defences aimed to prevent vehicles from getting ashore here. (Author)

Now half-hidden in the undergrowth (on right), this pillbox still guards the point at which the railway crosses Portscreek, just north of Hilsea Lines. Another pillbox survives at Eastney swimming pool. Others in the area have been destroyed since the war. (Author)

This brick building at Farlington was one of the control shelters for the Hayling Island and Langstone Harbour bombing decoys. The principle was that once an air raid began, fires would be started to distract the attackers. This worked on the night of 17-18 April 1941, when the vast majority of bombs intended for Portsmouth were dropped on the Starfish site (as the decoys were known) on Hayling Island – although that was no consolation for those killed there. (Author)

The D-Day Museum and Overlord Embroidery, on the Southsea seafront, tells the story of D-Day from a national perspective, and also records the events of wartime Portsmouth. It is run by Portsmouth City Council as part of Portsmouth Museums & Records Service. Nearby on the seafront is the city's D-Day memorial. (PMRS)

# Other local titles published by The History Press

## Plymouth at War
DEREK TAIT

During the Second World War, Plymouth suffered some of the worst Blitz damage in the country. Bustling streets such as Bedford Street, George Street and Old Town Street were totally destroyed, while popular stores including Dingles, Pophams, Boots and Woolworth were reduced to rubble. Illustrated with over 220 archive photographs and documents, *Plymouth at War* offers a unique record of the wartime history of Plymouth.

0 7524 3850 6

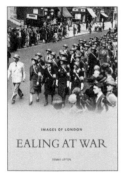

## Ealing at War
DENNIS UPTON

Published on the sixtieth anniversary of the end of the Second World War, in association with the Ealing Library and Information Service, *Ealing at War* offers a unique record of the wartime history of the people of Ealing, Acton and Southall. Illustrated with 100 archive photographs and documents, the book recalls life on the Home Front, drawing on the first-hand accounts of those who were present during those dangerous years.

0 7524 3518 3

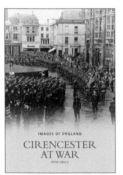

## Cirencester at War
PETER GRACE

*Cirencester at War* is a pictorial record of the main events of the Second World War as they impacted on the town of Cirencester and its surrounding district. Illustrated with over 200 old photographs and documents, the book gives an insight into wartime life with its tragedy, heroism, austerity and, of course, humour. Recalling upon an important era in Cirencester's history it will bring back wartime memories for many people.

0 7524 3477 2

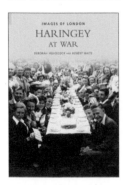

## Haringey at War
DEBORAH HEDGECOCK AND ROBERT WAITE

This collection of photographs from Bruce Castle Museum offers a pictorial record of the wartime history of the London Borough of Haringey, highlighting important events for the former boroughs of Tottenham, Hornsey and Wood Green, as well as life-changing events for its residents. Aspects of everyday life are also featured, from the destruction of homes and the trials of rationing, to land girls, Belgian refugees and air-raid shelters.

0 7524 3297 4

If you are interested in purchasing other books published by The History Press, or in case you have difficulty finding any of our books in your local bookshop, you can also place orders directly through our website
www.thehistorypress.co.uk